The Essesntial Herb Gardening Handbook

How Any Home Cook Can Grow Flavors from Around the World

Daniel I Stein

RMC Publishers

© Copyright 2022 - All rights reserved.

It is not legal to reproduce, duplicate, or transmit any part of this document in either electronic means or in printed format. Recording of this publication is strictly prohibited and any storage of this document is not allowed unless with written permission from the publisher except for the use of brief quotations in a book review.

Contents

Introduction	5
1. Planning your Herb Garden	13
2. What Type of Herb Garden is Right for Me	23
3. Twenty Popular Herbs to Grow	41
4. How to Sow, Propagate and Divide Herbs	83
5. Soil Improvement and Companion Planting	91
6. History and Basic Techniques	99
7. What Could Go Wrong? (and how to fix it)	127
8. Cooking with Herbs	155
Conclusion	165
Glossary	167

Introduction

Flowers are fantastic. They look lovely, smell nice, and I can definitely see the appeal. But once you have grown your flowers, and they are sitting there in a nice vase or pot, you're kind of at the end, aren't you?

At least for me, there's only so much looking and appreciating and rose-smelling I can do before those flowers start blending into the scenery; I start forgetting to water them, and then one day, there just happens to be a dead brown mess on the windowsill.

Herbs, on the other hand, are a different story. You're not planting a decoration; you're planting food, or more accurately, planting flavors. At the end of this journey, you'll have dozens of recipes, meals, and experiences to enjoy, and of course, most herbs produce flowers too. You also won't have to give up your entire yard or balcony; just a few pots, or planters, or a windowsill is all you need.

Introduction

The promise at the end of herb gardening is just that little bit of extra motivation to keep things exciting, and to see your garden through the seasons.

In your dream herb garden, does the sun pour in a sunny window, with the light shining on a row of green tips with aromatic scents? Do sweet-smelling herbs thrive in pots on your windowsill all winter long?

Do you reach over while you're cooking and cut a sprig of rosemary. Or pinch a few leaves of cilantro on the spur-of-the-moment? Or do you have a cabinet full of fresh and dried herbs that you have grown yourself?

No matter what your dream herb garden looks like, this book will help you devise a plan for your herb garden, guide you through choosing your herbs, and teach you how to use these unique plants in your cooking.

Think of this book as having two friendly neighbors.

The first is a gardener who knows exactly when to add fertilizer for the beans to grow well, which seeds are the best for the local soil, or where to put sunflowers to catch as much light as possible.

The second is a chef who knows exactly what spices to pair together, always has the perfect twist to brighten up an old family recipe, and understands how to use fresh ingredients to the most impressive effect. This book will guide you through selecting and planting a set of herbs to suit your taste so that you will always have the flavors you need on hand to enhance your culinary masterpieces.

Let's start with the first questions new gardeners often ask.

Introduction

Don't worry about getting all of the answers now. These first questions are just to get you thinking and to get your creative juices flowing. After that, we're going to go through everything step-by-step, and by the time you finish this book, you'll know everything you need to create your perfect herb garden.

1. How much space do I need to grow herbs?

The short answer is you can make any space suitable to grow herbs.

First, look at the space where you're thinking of planting your herb garden. If it is a windowsill, is the sun direct? What time of the day does it get sun? What size of pots or containers could fit here? If it's a balcony, is it sunny or shaded? Is there room to build a planter? Is there a shelf or a table to put pots on? Is there concrete on the surface or a grass lawn, a garden shed, or just a pile of junk? Take a few pictures and give yourself a day or two to imagine the space filled with herbs of your choice. Next, look at Chapter 1 for more help designing and planning your herb garden. In Chapter 2, you can read about herb gardens that have worked around the world for many gardeners. See if any of these gardens appeal to you, then check if you have a suitable climate, soil, and sunlight and try one!

2. How important is the climate for my plants?

Next, think of herbs growing in your chosen space and the environmental conditions you will provide. For example, there may be frost in certain areas overnight or in winter. Or maybe it is desert-like in summer so that plants may need lots of water? What is your annual rainfall? Will herbs get waterlogged if it rains every day? Most plants enjoy bright sunshine and warm weather, but you will be surprised at how many herbs also thrive in part sun, part shade when the hottest afternoon sun is glaring down! Mint is one of these. It seems to

Introduction

gasp in hot sunshine, so this is a plant to give some welcome shade so that you can enjoy peppermint tea or mint in roasted dishes.

3. How much light and how much room will my plants need?

If your proposed herb garden is going to be in pots, will you construct a special area for your herbs? Is there a large tree in your garden that may compete with your little herbs for light and soil? Are there any high walls that shelter the area from the wind? Some herbs like shelter, and some are pretty used to windy coastal shorelines. If you have walls, will they throw a lot of shade? Check if something shades parts of your patio, the backyard, or the balcony where you will place your plants. Annual herbs grow happily in pots and you can re-seed them each spring, but perennial herbs (which can stay outdoors in winter, too) need enough soil and space to thrive. All of these factors will determine where you should place your pots, planters, or herb garden.

To get started, snap a photo of your future herb gardening space in the early morning, at midday, and again in the late afternoon. Start noticing where the sun arrives first thing in the morning and at what time the light disappears. In spring and summer, this will be where you put a chair with a coffee to welcome in the day. You are gaining knowledge about what time the sun rises, and at what time the shade hits certain areas of your garden. The pictures will enable you to draw in plants over the areas to visualize what type of plant will grow best where.

To keep track of your progress, at this stage, I usually tell people to take these pictures and to start making your gardening journal, so take down some notes.

- What areas get full sun all day, partial sun for a few hours, or no sun at all?

Introduction

- Are there nearby buildings or trees that shade or shelter certain spots from the wind or rain?
- What is the temperature like, does the spot get frost in the morning, is it covered from the rain, or is it indoors and next to a drafty window or a warm space heater?

I thoroughly recommend recording your notes and ideas, including any herb gardens you visit and would like to copy. If you add photos, this becomes a treasured memento of your gardening journey. When you look back at the empty place when you started, you will notice a considerable change in your herb garden over a season. These photos are your reminder of success (and maybe failures) so that you can learn and improve. Now you have an idea of what is possible in your space, let's look at another critical question.

4. What kind of soil do herbs need to thrive?

The next important factor for plants is the soil in which they grow. In a pot, you can control this completely, and if these are annual herbs like basil, parsley, or cilantro, then you can change the soil in pots whenever you need to. However, if these plants will live there for a longer period like sage, rosemary, or thyme, you need to consider what conditions these plants have in their native Mediterranean landscapes. Some grow in dry, impoverished soils, so don't worry if your garden soil isn't all that fertile. It may be precisely what your herb needs. You can always add fertilizer and other nutrients to boost your soil's fertility at a later date. Read Chapter 4 for more information about soil, composting, and improving your soil.

5. Which herbs grow well together?

We will look at combinations of herbs that grow well together. Companion planting is the term for growing plants side by side that will benefit each other, or if one is being used as a sacrificial

Introduction

offering to pests so that your precious herbs do not get targeted. For example, nasturtiums are often grown next to other plants simply because aphids love them! Aphids will ignore every other plant if nasturtiums are close by. The cheerful blooms of nasturtiums can be eaten in salads, and their delicate little leaves are also edible, but if they distract pests away from your chosen herb, even better. See Chapters 3 and 4 for detailed information about companion planting and the needs of 20 of the most popular garden herbs.

6. What kind of herb garden should I grow? What kind of herbs are best for the foods I like to cook and eat?

Maybe you envisage an Italian garden, planning meals with basil in pesto, accompanied by tomatoes, marjoram, and cilantro? Mediterranean perennial herbs can be grown well together, such as sage, rosemary, thyme, and lavender. Many combinations of herbs can grow well together, and only you can decide which combinations will suit your space, climate, and taste. The time you have available is another factor in planning your garden. Are you going to be watering before work or before taking children to school and mulching plants to improve fertility, or do you fancy a low-maintenance herb garden that looks after itself? Are you keen to encourage beneficial wildlife into your garden by growing flowers to attract bees and butterflies? In this book, we will examine various options so that you can make an informed choice. Chapter 5 explains the uses of herbs in cooking. Chapter 6 will delve into the history of herbs grown for aromatic or medicinal use, the medieval cottage garden, and some more unusual herbs and recipes to try.

7. How do you use herbs properly?

This book will help you as a complete beginner and guide you as you learn more about the needs of individual herbs and how you can use them. Nothing is set in stone. If your herbs are in pots

Introduction

and you are not keen on one herb, you can just try a different combination the following year. If your herb garden is in a planter, you can remove plants for indoor winter use or decide which herbs may prefer another space after one season. If you've planted annual herbs, you can dry their leaves for winter use, make herb oils for yourself and your friends, and you can leave the perennial herbs in situ until the next active growing season. Some herbs are super easy to propagate or plant from seed. Save the seeds, dry the herbs and then give these as gifts to other gardeners.

It is helpful to find another keen gardener or join a gardening club, and this is a great way to get advice, swap plants, and maybe participate in a community project working with groups that need keen gardeners. Chapter 6 will guide you through some unusual herbs you can try once you have gained confidence with your first herbs. Chapter 4 will provide valuable propagation methods, how to remove your delicate plants indoors for winter, and how to save seeds and dry herb leaves for use in colder seasons.

In addition, Chapter 7 offers ways to deal with common problems and pests which affect herbs. For example, why are my basil leaves turning yellow? Or what's eating my cilantro? You can try organic cures and ancient tricks that will attract the right pollinator bees but keep the aphids and pests at bay. In midsummer, you can enjoy fresh basil chopped into tomatoes and salads. When the fall arrives, you can admire the dried herbs you've hung in a shady patch in your house, relax in sweet-smelling homemade lavender oil in your bathtub or nip out to a rosemary bush and pick a few leaves to add to soup or casseroles. Enjoy!

Chapter 1
Planning your Herb Garden

IF THIS IS YOUR FIRST ATTEMPT AT GARDENING, THEN LET'S assume that herb plants are a bit like humans. Like us, they need food, warmth, water, and shelter, and different plants have different preferences. Like humans, some plants crave the hot sun, while others prefer to bask in the shade during the afternoon heat. Some prefer rich, deep soil, while others can survive in the impoverished, dusty ground.

Food for your herb plants is the soil they grow in and any extra fertilizers you provide.

Warmth is usually provided by the sun but can also come from a greenhouse or a more sheltered spot indoors or an area with stones, which attracts heat and loses it slowly as the sun sets; these all make a cozy place for plants.

Water is essential for germinating most seeds, and without enough moisture, your herbs will die. On the other hand, too much water and their roots get waterlogged, so you need to understand how much water is correct for the herbs you choose. It is usually best to plant herbs with similar needs together.

Shelter is the last on the list, and remember that you will see smaller plants using shrubs as protection in the wild. You may be familiar with the way bluebells choose to grow in woodlands in the late spring, protected by the cover of the larger trees above but also making full use of the available light before the summer leaf cover fully shades them.

Choosing your Herbs

Are you familiar with all the herbs you can grow? Do you want to try particular ones? Chapter 3 of this book gives you a list of 20 popular herbs with detailed instructions on their ideal planting conditions. You can go straight there now or read on for some factors to consider first.

For example, an herb like basil needs deep, rich soil and lots of water because, in the countryside where they grow wild, that's what they are used to. If you choose basil and want to try other herbs like rosemary, thyme, and French tarragon (the Mediterranean herbs), be aware that these herbs would probably be better off in a different pot. Mediterranean herbs often start their lives on the edge of sunny, arid cliffs close to the sea, where the soil tends to be sandy and not so rich. These herbs have long, deep roots so that they cannot be uprooted easily by windy breezes but also so they can dig deep to find any water that is deep underground. So if you want basil and one of these Mediterranean herbs, you may want to place them either in separate pots or in a different section of your herb garden.

Let's go over some things to consider when deciding where to plant our herbs.

Where should they be planted?

Planning your garden means deciding if your herbs will all grow in pots or if you want to design a particular part of the garden in soil for your herbs. You may already know not to plant sage close to other herbs, and there are groups of herbs that do well together. If you grow tomatoes in pots, you can also pop a basil plant in there. Cilantro, marjoram, and chives are a good match for tomatoes too, as they all like a bit of shade in the afternoon, and the larger tomato plant will provide that.

POTS

Pots are a trick most experienced gardeners know. You can start seeding all your herbs indoors in pots early in spring and then put them outside when all danger of frost has gone. The pots can enjoy the long, balmy days in the summer sunshine, and then you can bring some of them back indoors when the fall arrives. This way, you can have basil all year round in your kitchen, as well as parsley and chives. Some herbs like tarragon, lovage, and mint will die back naturally in colder temperatures, but if you want some of these during the winter, you can dry their leaves.

So are you planning to grow your herbs in pots indoors, outdoors, or both?

If your herbs are going to grow on a sunny windowsill or a balcony, make sure they get lots of direct sunlight and plenty of fresh air. However, it might infrequently rain in summer in their natural environment, so my advice is not to overwater them. Rainwater often does the job for you. As a general rule, indoor herbs tend to get overwatered.

Your herbs will provide you with gorgeous aromatic smells as you walk past, which will also brighten your mood in a work area. Humanity has used herbs like this for centuries. Think of lavender bath oil and rose-scented soap, and most people will instantly relax, which is precisely what these scents do for the human body.

The soil in pots is usually sufficient for only one growing season. After that, you may need to add a top mulch or a layer of compost, leaf mulch, or ash to the pots to keep plants going. All of these settle quickly with watering, but a problem with soil in pots is that soil gets compacted over time and that the tap water used is full of chlorine which can start to build up in the soil. As an alternative, you could save any available rainwater from roof collection into a water barrel. Try to ensure that water barrels are covered though because this is the perfect breeding ground for mosquitoes in temperate climates.

Be careful with annual herbs in pots that try to flower too soon. Usually, this happens because all the goodness in the pot has been used up. The plant's instinct is to turn to seed as soon as soil nutrients are depleted, there is a lack of available water, or the temperatures drop.

Re-pot any herbs immediately when you can see roots coming out the end of the pot. It's also a good idea to add more soil to pots when you take them indoors for winter so that they have enough energy to get through the colder season. Many perennial herbs go dormant in winter when the weather turns chillier, but they are alive and will spring back into life when the warmer air of spring comes around.

PLANTERS OR BEDS

If you plan to build a herb garden either as a raised bed or in the soil, then choose an area that gets a lot of sunshine as most herbs thrive in bright sunshine. Basil, parsley, chives, sage, rosemary, and thyme all love direct sunlight, and they will reward you with abundant foliage for your efforts. Indoors, as long as they get some sunshine every day, your herbs will be fine, but you will probably not be rewarded by the enormous bunches of fresh foliage they can produce outdoors. Some exceptions to this rule do exist – for example; mint prefers some shade. However, note that mint is an herb that needs to be contained because it spreads like crazy and can take over your whole herb garden.

Raised beds are fantastic for people who cannot kneel or whose backs need some tender care. A raised bed for herbs is perfect for a community garden or shared space because it allows a wide range of people to enjoy it. A raised bed is the ideal solution if herb gardeners need some support, such as a walker or a wheelchair. The deep soil makes it very fertile, the height makes it accessible, and you can plant rows of herbs so that everybody can pick some tasty leaves. Making a raised bed from bricks allows you to place all the tools you need and seeds or pots on the edge of the bed, as well as that welcome cup of tea all gardeners seem to enjoy while they admire the results of their hard work.

MAKING A NEW BED IN SOIL

If you can, place a cover over the area in the months prior to planting to warm it up and kill off any weeds. Prepare your ground well by digging out any weeds and their roots so that you are starting with fresh, weed-free soil. Bindweed and dandelion roots left in the soil tend to spread like crazy, so if you see long, thick white roots resembling string, this is Bindweed or Morning Glory, which has fantastic tubular white flowers. Lovely as these are, they spread by underground roots, so take out every piece you see and dispose of them. Do not put these segments of root in your compost bin. Each little segment is viable as a plant due to the root suckers you will notice; it is a complete triumph of nature's ability to propagate new plants. Shame it's not a herb! However, these roots will happily absorb all the rich goodness of your compost heap, so get rid of them another way.

One option is to dump the whole lot (roots, leaves, flowers) into a bucket of water and let them rot for 4-5 days. Strain the resulting mixture into a watering can or bottle as a fertilizer for tomatoes or some of your hungry herbs later. Dig deep to remove any long roots of dandelions, or you will see these in your herb garden for many years to come. However, although classed as a weed, dandelion does provide beneficial color and nectar for bees in spring. Dandelion leaf tea is drunk all over Europe. You can even use these dandelion leaves to make homemade fertilizer for your other plants – see Chapter 2 for details of nutrients these "weeds" can provide.

The final question is, has this area been dug before?

If you have lived here for years, you will know the answer, but if you just moved in, it is an excellent idea to discover if this area was used to grow anything in the past. Pests love soil that has been undisturbed, and a multitude of lurking slugs and snails may be licking their lips at the idea of the tasty herb supper you are about to plant. However, another consideration comes from what farmers call crop rotation. You may remember this from history or geography or botany lessons. The basic idea is that to grow healthy plants; you should not grow the same crop in the same soil year after year. See more about this in Chapter 3. For now, let's assume this is year 1 in your herb planning for your garden or pots.

It is essential in designing your herb bed to think about each herb and how much space it will need. Next, a word about how long your plants will stay in the ground and how experienced gardeners describe this.

How long will they last?

What exactly are annual, biennial, and perennial herbs?

Parsley, basil, cilantro, and marjoram all grow well together. These are all annual herbs; this means you plant them, they grow, and they live only for one growing season. These herbs die back naturally at the start of the cold weather in the fall or winter, and the seeds they make may fall to the ground and start to grow as new plants when the soil gets warmer the following year.

Some herbs are biennial; this means they grow well from seed in their first year, then flower in the second year and die back after this. Typical flowers that do this are foxgloves and Sweet William. Biennial herbs are more unusual – chervil is one example; it grows well in the first year, but it usually dies back after flowering in the second year. However, chervil will seed itself in the second year if you leave the plant in the same place, and there will always be plants if you allow it to self-seed. It is a vibrant herb for salads, providing an unusual aniseed taste. It is used (like Sweet Cicely) in cooking to balance bitter plants like rhubarb and cuts down on the amounts of added sugar you use. It likes semi-shade, so that it can be planted under a raspberry or blackcurrant bush.

Perennial herbs start pretty small but gradually grow larger and spread, often turning woody as they do. In hot climates, this is a method of propagation. Many of the pieces of branches knocked off by animals or wind will sprout roots where they land, making an entirely new plant. They are usually frost-tolerant, and you can plant them from seeds, cuttings, or small plants. They grow over many years and will last in your garden for five years, and often a lot longer.

Lavender is like this. You have probably seen large, overgrown plants with thick stems and felt maybe it was time to prune these branches at times. Sage and rosemary do the same and can spread into substantial shrubs, which may cause a space problem if they overhang some of the annuals in your herb garden. Sage is a perennial herb that is also notorious among experienced gardeners because it tends to kill off anything that grows too close to it. Its delicious smell is fabulous in cooking but lethal for some other plants. Strawberries are an exception, and borage flowers love being next to sage. Thyme does not grow as tall as sage and rosemary, but it does have beautiful flowers! Bees also love rosemary, sage, and thyme, and they snack on their attractive flowers as they pass. Sage and rosemary spread a lot, but the thyme bush is small and compact, and it allows you to pick fresh thyme whenever you need it. This plant survives snow in England, so unless your weather is extreme, your thyme plant should be fine. All of these perennial herbs come back year after year, flowering in early summer and attracting bees and beneficial insects to your herb garden.

Big perennial shrubs prefer a bit of space to grow – see soil, expected spread, and watering needs in detail for each herb in Chapter 5.

How much water do they need?

Think about watering them too. If you plan to use a watering can, make sure your water supply isn't too far away. If the herbs are indoors in less accessible spots or outdoors, you may not notice a herb drooping, so check them every few days. You probably will be picking them frequently in summer, or you could enlist the help of a younger gardener to take on the task for pocket money.

The Essesntial Herb Gardening Handbook

By now, have you gotten a clearer picture of your gardening space?

- Will your herbs grow indoors in small pots, or do you plan to grow these herbs outdoors in larger pots or beds? Will you create a raised bed?
- Is there enough sunlight? Shelter? And will you be able to water them easily?
- Have you chosen a selection of seeds yet? If not, you can move on to the herb details in Chapter 3 for help.

This is not a recipe book, but I can certainly point you towards some of the delightful tastes herbs provide in kitchens around the world (Chapter 8) and encourage you to try at least one unusual one. Chapter 2 describes the herbs that people use and grow worldwide from Canada to Latin America, from Asia and Africa to Europe.

Chapter 2
What Type of Herb Garden is Right for Me

This chapter will first examine 10 of the most popular herbs for any herb garden or windowsill for the absolute beginner. These are 10 excellent choices that are popular, easy to grow, and are very versatile in the kitchen. After looking at these 10 herbs, you can then read about different styles of herb gardens around the world.

After seeing the other types of herb gardens, you may decide to add some exotic herbs to your list and adapt some less common flavors into your cooking.

Remember, while these herbs go well together in these cuisines, that doesn't necessarily mean that they will grow well together in a pot.

The beginner's (Italian) herb garden

Useful for anyone, and benefits almost any cooking style.

1. **Basil**. This staple herb from Italy offers fresh green leaves to eat raw or chopped into tomato salads. It is also the main ingredient for pesto sauce. It is usually grown as an annual herb, and most supermarkets sell pots of basil for cooks to use. You can use the leaves and flowers in your recipes.
2. **Bay leaves** are often picked from a shrub in your backyard and then dried for use by hanging them on some string in a cool area that does not get bright direct sunshine. Once dried, bay leaves can be added to soups, sauces, and casseroles, where the flavor of the leaves adds a subtle herb taste.
3. **Chives** add an onion-like flavor to many dishes. They can be eaten raw or chopped into dishes and cooked slightly. Garlic chives are somewhat thicker and have a stronger taste.
4. **Cilantro** is easy to grow but quick to go to seed. In cooking, you can use both leaves and flowers as well as the seeds. Indian cuisine uses ground coriander (the seeds) as an ingredient for several dishes.
5. **Garlic** is very easy to grow and is a tiny miracle for younger gardeners who plant one clove and dig up an entire bulb. Garlic is traditionally associated with French cuisine, but it is used worldwide and comes with a range of health benefits. See more about this in Chapter 6.
6. **Marjoram** is a Mediterranean herb and spreads like crazy in a herb garden. It is a favorite for bees to visit, so if you want to feed the wildlife or get some flowers pollinated, this is one to include. It adds a subtle taste to

many Mediterranean dishes and is widely used in recipes.
7. **Parsley** is famous for being an ingredient of parsley sauce, a white sauce used to flavor fish, and it comes in 2 types; flat-leaved and moss curled. This herb is very difficult to germinate from seed, requiring heat and moisture, so if you want an easy start to your herb garden, buy some pots to start you off.
8. **Thyme** is a perennial herb, that is, one that grows for many years. Its native habitat is on dry cliffs, where it provides bees with welcome nectar and provides any visitor to the garden a delicious scent as they walk by. It likes soil that is not too rich, loves the sun, and does not need much watering. An easy starter herb!
9. **Rosemary** is another perennial herb, and once planted, it will spread quite wide, so allow it plenty of space in your herb garden.
10. **Sage** is used fresh and dried and adds a delicious rich flavor to stews and winter casseroles.

Almost every single herb in the Beginner garden plan is used in Italian cooking, from bay leaves to basil, marjoram, chives, rocket, various salad leaves, and tomatoes. Home of pizza and pasta, Italy is also the inventor of pesto sauce, which is available around the world and in many variations. In Italy, the details of the family pesto recipe may be a closely-held secret. See Chapter 6 for using these Italian herbs to make pesto, some information about canning tomatoes and other produce with herb flavoring, etc. Olives are not herbs, but they are very Italian, and olive oil (organic if possible) can be used for herb oils and in Italian dishes. We do not include growing pine nuts for use in pesto, but if you have the space and climate, this is a challenge for your future herb garden once this one is established.

Essential herbs to include in your Italian herb garden:

Basil, garlic, chives, thyme, marjoram, sage, rosemary, pine nuts, bay leaves, peppers, chili peppers, and of course, tomatoes! See how to grow all of these herbs in detail in Chapter 3.

If you're unsure what kind of garden you want, these 10 herbs would be an excellent start. But if you have a favorite type of cuisine, take a look and see if any of these themed herb gardens would work for you.

(If the herbs have already been described, I will not include them in detail below.)

The French herb garden

Next, let's move on to the herbs found in parts of France, which is colder in the north with a warmer, temperate climate near the Mediterranean sea in the south, where the soil may be more sandy for your herbs. If you look for pre-mixed herb packages in stores, two French mixes are almost always included. The *Fines Herbes* and the *Herbes de Provence* collections are a reference for French cooks, and their fame has spread to other countries that enjoy French cooking.

France is famous worldwide for its champagne grapes, distinctive cuisine, olives, cheese, and patisserie pastry shops. It is also home to the renowned herb liqueur, the pea-green colored Chartreuse. Carthusian monks are reputed to have followed a recipe for "the elixir of long life" using 130 herbs and plants to make a medicinal alcoholic tonic in the monastery since 1737. You can read more about herbs used in history and how they control or aid recovery from various ailments in Chapter 6. For now, let's look at herbs necessary for inclusion in any French herb garden.

Essential herbs to include in your French herb garden:

The Essesntial Herb Gardening Handbook

1. **French Tarragon** is frequently used in many French recipes, but it is not a common herb in many countries due to the difficulty of sourcing the plant. It is very different from Russian Tarragon, which you can grow from seed but does not have the same flavor despite the name, whereas the delicate flavor of French Tarragon can only be added to your garden by getting a plant. The reason for this is that this herb rarely flowers, and even if it does, the seeds may not grow the same as the mother plant. The propagation of this herb commonly happens by cutting a stem, popping it in water, and then saving this indoors over winter. You can pot on tarragon when the roots show in water, and it can be planted outdoors again the following summer. Root divisions are also possible in early spring, but you need an actual plant to start with. This herb is fond of warm conditions, so if frost is expected in your garden, ensure that you keep it indoors in cold seasons after the fall arrives. If you have French Tarragon, make a few cuttings in any case, as it is temperamental. Having a few backup plants in pots is an excellent way to have a supply of this delicate flavor for culinary use. Do not plant it outside until all danger of frost has passed.
2. **Rosemary**, **thyme**, and **sage** are essential components of French herb gardens, so make sure you include these perennial herbs. Once planted, they will happily remain in your garden for several years. See detailed instructions for growing them in Chapter 3.
3. **Fennel** is a herb that should definitely grace any French herb garden. It is one of the ingredients of the infamous absinthe drink, which was drunk in vast quantities by many famous artists during the Belle Époque. At that time, the herb-infused drink was a treatment for epilepsy, kidney stones, and a multitude of others.

Vincent van Gogh, Pablo Picasso, and Henri Toulouse-Lautrec were said to enjoy the taste of the green mixture. However, modern doctors might disagree with the effect of including wormwood as an ingredient because nowadays, it is known to induce hallucinations! So although wormwood is NOT recommended, fennel is a valuable herb. The leaves can be eaten, and its seeds frequently flavor staple dishes in any French café. One word of advice with growing fennel. If grown very close to dill, the two herbs cross breed and create combinations of herbs with unpredictable tastes, so avoid placing these two herbs close to one another.
4. **Chives** add an onion flavor to salads, and they are commonly an addition to many white sauces for poultry and meat. They are also utilized in cold herb kinds of butter used to flavor fish dishes. Finally, chives are also one of the essential four herbs used in so many dishes in France called "Fine Herbs".
5. **Chervil** is included in Herbes de Provence as well as being an ingredient in salads and used as a natural sweetener of rhubarb and sour fruits.
6. **Herbs de Provence** is a mix of herbs used dried in recipes to add flavor to meat, poultry, fish, and vegetables which originates in the Provence area of France, where these herbs grow in abundance. Essential herbs included are fennel, marjoram, parsley, rosemary, tarragon, and thyme. You can also add basil, bay leaves, savory, chervil, sage, oregano, mint, and even the flowers of lavender.

The Spanish herb garden

In Spanish cooking, the main ingredients besides the herbs include olive oil, various kinds of vinegar, and dressings. Like

The Essesntial Herb Gardening Handbook

other Mediterranean countries, Spain produces olives and olive oil, peppers, and some unusual herbs. For example, Spanish chorizo sausage has many herbs hardly known outside the country, yet the sausage is extremely popular. Secret recipes kept by the Spanish! This is the home of the paella; the classic seafood rice cooked to perfection with saffron. Although strictly not a herb, ñora is a round, ball-shaped pepper which is the secret ingredient only a Spanish cook knows! It is prepared by being first dried in direct sunlight and then ground into a seasoning. Its distinctive flavor is not well known outside Spain and is certainly worth tasting if you visit. Spain's traditional chorizo sausage owes much of its characteristic flavor to this herb, and ñora is added to patatas bravas, the spicy potatoes offered in tapas bars, and sometimes the whole plant is served as a vegetable after being cooked with garlic. Gazpacho is the refreshing cold summer soup first made to use up a glut of tomatoes, and today it is one of the most famous Spanish dishes on a hot summer's day, and it is flavored with garlic and pepper. Read on to see the herbs and spices included in traditional Spanish cooking.

1. **Saffron** is a traditional herb prepared from a particular type of crocus flower and collected painstakingly by Spanish farmers every year. These petals cause the rice to be tinted yellow shades through to maroon color in paella, the national seafood dish, and soups and sauces. Saffron is grown in La Mancha in Spain, and this spice is comparable to the price of gold when it is produced.
2. **Bay leaf** is grown as a small shrub and can even grow to tree size in the right conditions. The leaves are picked and dried, then hung until needed in the kitchen. You can dry them and store them in a herb jar in your kitchen.
3. **Garlic** is an essential Spanish ingredient for almost

every dish. It grows in bulbs, and one or two of these is enough to season a dish to perfection. Super easy to grow, this herb will survive frost, snow, and any conditions your local climate will throw at it.
4. **Ñora** is grown in Valencia on the west coast of Spain and is also known as **pimentón**. Columbus supposedly brought the first one back from Latin America, and he donated it to monks in the Yuste monastery. From this monastery garden, it traveled to La Nora in Murcia in the south of Spain. Typically dried and used as a powder, this is an essential dried plant seasoning for many Spanish dishes such as chorizo and is the secret ingredient that not many people know about!
5. **Oregano** is a small herb with tasty leaves which can be eaten fresh off the bush, but its delicate flavor escapes easily into a cooked dish. This herb is used in France, Italy, and Portugal as well as Spain and Greece.
6. **Chili pepper** is used sparingly in most Spanish dishes, and when it is too hot, the Spanish will complain saying it is picante. Chopped, it is added to dishes and cooked in stews.
7. **Nutmeg** (*Myristica fragrans*) and **cinnamon** (*Cinnamomum verum*), are used widely in Spanish cooking but are usually imported from India, Indonesia, and the West Indies. Both arrived with the return of the conquistadors to Spain after their long journeys trying to explore the New World. There is a rich tradition of use of these two in Spanish kitchens. The seeds of nutmeg are used in cooking, and you need to grate the nut to release the flavor in cooking. Cinnamon is edible tree bark from a variety of the Laurel family grown in Indonesia and Malaysia. These are not actually herbs, and unless you live in a hot climate you are unlikely to

be able to grow these, but they are essential tastes in Spanish cuisine.

Herbs from Greece, Turkey, and Lebanon

This is another Mediterranean herb garden similar to those used in Spain. However, the Greeks experimented by adding herbs and resin to wines which transformed into the retsina we recognize and relish on streetside tavernas on visits to Greece. Mastic is a cream-colored resin that grows near the Aegean sea on some Greek islands, which adds the famous taste to retsina, the national wine. The flavor of this drink is unique and, strangely enough, often disappoints if taken home and drunk outside of the Greek air and atmosphere.

1. **Dill** is a favorite herb here, and other herbs include **oregano**, **parsley**, and **marjory**.
2. **Nutmeg**, like in Spain, is also a common ingredient.
3. **Bay leaves** are frequently used in Greek cooking, and **oregano** and chopped mint add taste to many regional dishes. Remember that tasty bay leaves must be dried before you use them.
4. Greek seasoning you find in the supermarket is a mix of oregano, **garlic**, and onion powder mixed with dill and bay leaves, and sometimes mint.
5. **Mint** is often added to cooling dishes like tzatziki, which is a yogurt accompaniment to meat. Mint also features in delicious sweet desserts.
6. The seeds of **thyme** and **fennel** are used a lot, and olive oil is the main ingredient in many dishes.
7. **Cloves** are imported and used with many dishes, and parsley is occasionally used, particularly as a herb garnish.

8. **Cilantro** has been used in Greece for centuries, adding its sweet taste to various dishes.
9. Alongside mastic, which grows in the Aegean, pine honey is another exotic taste found in Greek cooking, and thyme-flavored honey is also popular. Honey is often added to Greek breakfast selections to flavor natural yogurt.
10. Citrus trees are abundant in Greece, and lemon often features as a garnish and a flavor.
11. Eggplant is vital in dishes like Moussaka, which offers layers of cheese and eggplant with meat and herbs. Zucchini flowers are a specialty, usually filled with generous helpings of rice, herbs, and spices.
12. Vine leaves are also cooked in these countries, and "Dolmades" in Greece is a lift straight from Turkish, where "dolma" means to fill. The taste of these leaves combined with herbs and spices makes them a very popular dish all over this region. Greek people often say that spring has arrived when they see fresh vine leaves being sold in markets, but they are not just available in the growing season either; the leaves are added to vinegar and dried to be used in every season. Dill, parsley, and lemon are the herbs and fruit grown in the region which are commonly added to dolmades.
13. Cheese is more often than not made from sheep's milk, where the land is not especially fertile for cattle. Feta cheese is a specialty in Greece and Turkey and is so well-known worldwide it hardly needs an introduction. Often served in feta cheese appetizers, with herbs to accompany it, including dill, parsley, and oregano, the cheese is usually mixed with a generous serving of olive oil. However, it is not the only available cheese, and if you visit, you will find a combination of cheeses you probably would only see in a New York deli! Ladotyn

cheese contains added olive oil, Graviera cheese with added thyme gives it a unique taste, and there is also a spreadable cheese called Katiki Domokou. Epiros cheese offers a salty, minty taste, so there are many herb-flavored cheese delights to try. A common use of herbs worldwide is to season meat dishes, and particularly in the north of Greece, the sweeter tasting, imported spices like cinnamon and cloves are added with local herbs.

14. **Parsley** is a typical garnish, and **tarragon** also features in this region's dishes, adding something extra to meat and chicken dishes and stews.

The Mexican herb garden

The Spanish conquistadors were amazed at the difference in the produce available in Mexico compared to their native country on their arrival. They saw many strange fruits and vegetables used in the Mexican dishes that are so familiar nowadays. For example, the avocado was a pear they had never seen, and cocoa was revered as a sacred drink the Spanish had never even imagined. Thanks to Mexican knowledge of the cacao plant, the world now enjoys hot chocolate. In Spain, it is enjoyed with a snack called churros.

Who has not heard of chile con carne? This super-hot mincemeat fried with red hot chili peppers is served in Mexican restaurants as the typical dish of this country. There are other famous dishes, such as guacamole, made of avocado, which calms down the hotter dishes common in Mexican cuisine, such as pozole rojo, the red stew that also utilizes the deep red chili peppers. This soup is usually accompanied by garnishes such as chopped radishes, cabbage, scallions, cilantro, and finally, the essential carbohydrate in Mexico: corn tortillas.

Herbs native to Mexico include **coriander**, **allspice**, **cloves**, **thyme**, **Mexican oregano**, **Mexican cinnamon**, and **cumin**. Other plants used are **Aloe Vera**, **Galangal root**, **Epazote**, and **chili pepper**, some of which were used as food but also as medicine.

Mexican oregano is not the same as the common oregano that is widely used in Europe and the Americas. This oregano has a slightly different flavor, and you should use less of it than you usually use because the taste is more intense.

Mint is widely used in dressings and drinks and often balances some of the heat in other dishes.

Herb gardens in India and Asia

The warmer climates found in both India and Asia offer a wider variety to choose from for your herb garden. Unusual herbs like **cinnamon** and **cloves** can grow in Indonesia, and **ginger** grows widely all over this part of the world. There are many ground and powdered flavors a visitor will recognize on the shelves of a supermarket here and others that we would find hard to recognize. In some areas of this region, **powdered mango**, **nutmeg**, and **lemongrass** grow.

Mystica fragrans is the tree that is the source for both **mace** and nutmeg. Nutmeg is the inner seed that is grated into cooking, and it grows inside another external layer (or aril) which is then ground into the herb we call mace. According to local knowledge, both of these herbs are said to aid digestion. Other medicinal uses in Asia for these two will be explored in Chapter 5.

Cinnamon comes from the Cinnamomum zeylanicum tree, and both trees grow in many parts of India, mainly in Kerala. These trees can also grow in the Tamil Nadu and Karnataka regions.

Cloves are flower buds of a tree in Indonesia, and they are exported widely because of their unique flavor. Clove trees need a lot of space as they can grow up to 40 feet. However, they are beautiful trees if you have the climate and lots of time! They will fruit for many years, some as long as 80 years.

You can grow almost anything here, and herbs can last all year round, providing you care for them. **Basil**, **cilantro**, **chives**, and **garlic** are all widely used to flavor many recipes as all of these herbs enjoy the hot weather and the direct sunlight that is on offer.

The Chinese herb garden

There are ingredients found in Chinese cooking which are not widely used in the West. Traditionally some of these are known as spices, not herbs, but as the origin is from plants that provide flavor to food, I will discuss one of these which the herb grower might not consider in other countries.

Ginger is not strictly a herb, but its roots are used to flavor food worldwide, and it grows well in Asia, where it is a common ingredient in cooking and present in the herb garden. It is slightly more challenging to grow than some leafy herbs, the plant has striking spiky dark green foliage, but it is the root we consume for culinary purposes. Even as a decorative plant, ginger is worth adding to your windowsill. If you're lucky, you may be able to eat a small section and then re-plant some of the remaining roots to grow again. Ginger also grows well in areas like conservatories, where it can have a deeper pot and will grow to a better height. The foliage is stunning, and you can eat your elegant plant roots from time to time, always allowing for enough root to allow the plant to survive.

African Herbs

The vast continent of Africa includes many types of climate, from the desert in Egypt to more verdant lands all along the Nile basin to sunny climates at the end of the continent in South Africa. So should we class cloves as a spice or a herb? Typical African herbs are **harissa**, **zanzibar**, **berbere**, **cloves**, **peri-peri** mix, and **grains of paradise**, which is counted as a spice, but as it comes from the grains of plants, I have included it as a herb. Some of these names are well known to Europeans, who travel to Morocco more frequently, and harissa is widely used in cooking and available to buy in markets. **Coconut** is not strictly classed as a herb either, rather a dried fruit. However, it is used in cooking, and its milk is a common ingredient in cuisine as far apart as from Africa to Brazil.

Herbs from Australia and New Zealand

Many of us associate Australia with tea tree oil. Other trees such as Eucalyptus were imported into the UK and Europe, where the gorgeous aroma added a wonderful scent as walkers passed by, and the elegance of the grown tree is a wonder! The leaves were used as herb oils in steam rooms and sauna buildings, where the infusion was reputed to help clear the air passageways and contribute to a calmer body in medicine. The legacy of the Aboriginal use of herbs before the arrival of colonizers to Australia included the use of plants such as native mint, which has approximately 90 species growing well in the wild. Ginger is also native to Australia and other parts of Asia, with hot temperatures ideal for cultivation. Often called Aniseed Myrtle, Myrtle is not the same as that grown in Europe, which is poisonous. There is a variety of Lemon Myrtle (Backhousia citriodora) classed as a rainforest tree native to Queensland.

The Essesntial Herb Gardening Handbook

In reality, an Australian Aboriginal herb garden would comprise all the land they covered on foot in their travels around the continent. Local knowledge of the siting of useful plants would have been recorded in the minds of adults who passed down both the location and the plant's use to the next generation. Although some knowledge has undoubtedly been lost, significant efforts have been made in conserving that knowledge for everyday use. When picking herbs like these in the wild, you must have an expert who can verify that the herbs you choose are safe for human consumption and their use and that picking them is legally permitted as some plants are protected by law. Buy seeds or plants from a reputable grower to grow in your own herb garden. Some to try:

1. **Native Ginger** (*Alpinia caerulea*). You will need warm conditions for this to grow well, but some European gardeners place them in warm greenhouses or indoors, where they are reported to thrive. The root is the part we know as ginger, and it is also dried for use in cooking.
2. **Bush Mint**. It is estimated that approximately 90 species of mint are native to Australia. Some types have gorgeous flowers, like those seen on traditional mint found in Europe, the US, and Canada. They make attractive hedge plants, and you can pick the leaves to use in tea and cooking.
3. **Lemon Myrtle** (*Backhousia citriodora*). This is more a tree than a herb, but if you live in Australia or a climate similar to Queensland, this tree is perfect! Traditionally it was used to cure headaches and also to cook with fish.
4. **Australian Ginger** (*Alpinia caerulea*). You can eat all parts of this native ginger plant, so this is an excellent addition to your herb garden if you can locate a root to start with. They can be divided as with other ginger, and a small piece of root is usually enough to begin with.

The tastiest edible parts are the new young shoots, similar to the bamboo shoots that grow in many parts of the world. Keep this plant moist – remember its native habitat is the rainforest and keep those conditions.

Now you have a good overview of herbs from all over the globe. In Chapter 3, there are detailed instructions on how to plant your herbs from seed, stem cuttings, or root pieces, what soil they need, and the optimum conditions to get you started.

IF YOU ARE ENJOYING '*THE ESSENTIAL HERB GARDENING Handbook*' please don't be shy about saying so! My goal is to help as many people as possible appreciate the environment around us, so feel free to share this book with your friends and family (and please leave a review at your preferred retailer).

Chapter 3
Twenty Popular Herbs to Grow

1. BASIL
2. BAY LEAF
3. CELERY
4. CHIVES
5. CILANTRO
6. DILL
7. FENNEL
8. GARLIC
9. LAVENDER
10. LEMON BALM
11. MARJORAM
12. MINT
13. OREGANO
14. PARSLEY
15. ROSEMARY
16. SAGE
17. SAVORY (SUMMER)
18. SAVORY (WINTER)
19. TARRAGON
20. THYME

Basil

This herb needs little introduction to herb lovers! Used all over the world in salads and cooking, its fame is often as the main ingredient in pesto sauce, that Italian favorite.

When to plant: Indoors in pots in late spring, plant outdoors in summer. Germination can be slow. Cover the pot with a plastic bag to keep it warm and then remove the bag when seeds sprout. For a winter crop, plant seeds again in August and take pots indoors for winter.

Best soil: Rich soil with plenty of humus, compost, and manure.

Best light: Full sun indoors; direct sunlight if outside.

Watering: Frequently; every day in hot water or if it flowers or goes to seed.

Plant next to: Tomatoes, chives, cilantro, marjoram, or in a greenhouse with these.

Harvesting: Pick leaves throughout the summer; plant new seeds in August for winter use indoors.

Cooking: Salads, Pesto, on pizzas, in pasta dishes, etc.

Problems: White flowers appear and the whole plant looks leggy. Trim off the flowers (you can eat them), water the plant more regularly, and give a top dressing of mulch. If you repot the whole plant you will give it a new life and more vigorous growth.

Bay Leaf

Bay is an evergreen shrub from the Laurel family and its leaves are dried for use in cooking. It likes shelter and grows tall, so a deep pot is required, or plant it in the ground if you can.

When to plant: Best to plant in a deep hole in autumn or spring outdoors.

Best soil: Rich soil with some lime content.

Best light: Full sun indoors; direct sunlight if outside.

Watering: Frequently once first planted. Then check weekly in summer.

Plant next to: It will grow tall but it smells fabulous next to other herbs. Rosemary and thyme are good companions.

Harvesting: Pick leaves when needed and hang them to dry. Use dried leaves in cooking.

Cooking: Dried leaves are used to add flavor to stews, soup, and cooked dishes and usually removed before serving.

Problems: This will grow into a tree if space permits. To stop it growing too tall, prune regularly and dry the leaves for culinary use.

Celery

Celery stems need to be fully covered to give them that yellowy-white color, so dig a deep trench and cover up the stems as they appear. When you pick a plant, make sure you cover up the stems of the plant next to it.

When to plant: Plant seeds in March/April indoors in pots and then plant outdoors in May/June, when there is no risk of frost. Prepare a trench outdoors then after your plant them in the ground, you can cover up the stems with earth as they appear.

Best soil: Celery grows for a long time in one place so needs lots of energy from the soil; make it as rich as you can. Manure the soil before planting and fertilize regularly during the growing summer season.

Best light: Bright sunshine for 40 weeks is needed for trench celery to mature so make sure the row is not shaded by summer crops.

Watering: Lots! Celery enjoys frequent watering and fertilizer. A very thirsty plant.

Plant next to: Give these plants lots of space and light and don't plant anything too close.

Harvesting: From October onwards. Pick stems from one plant, then cover up the next plant so that stems remain white.

Cooking: Use freshly cut in salads, raw for dipping into hummus instead of crackers, or as an addition to juices. Celery adds flavor to stocks and soups and we also use celery salt for seasoning.

Problems: Stems turn green when exposed to light. Cover them up well. These plants do not like frost or cold and if not watered and fertilized, your crop will be a disappointment. They take a long time to mature, this is not a plant for an impatient gardener.

Chives

Chives can be chopped into salads and sauces to add an onion flavor and garlic chives add a stronger, tangier taste. They are perennial – they will return each year once seeded.

When to plant: Tiny, little black chive seeds take ages to germinate so help them along with a sunny windowsill indoors and some central heating in the fall or spring. Then re-pot outdoors when the summer arrives.

Best soil: Rich soil or compost.

Best light: Full sun indoors; direct sunlight if outside.

Watering: Not usually necessary if planted in soil outdoors unless it is really hot and dry. Indoors, weekly should be enough but check the pot in warm weather.

Plant next to: You can plant them anywhere there is strong sunshine next to tomatoes, cilantro, and marjoram or in a flower bed. They have gorgeous purple flowers later in the summer.

Harvesting: Pick whenever you need them from late spring right through to the fall.

Cooking: A favorite in French cooking, chives are used in potato salads, omelets, and any recipe that needs an extra dash of fresh onion greenery.

Problems: Very few problems are reported with chives. Once established just add a top dressing of compost and water occasionally in warm weather.

Cilantro

In the UK, coriander is the name of the whole herb, whereas, in the US, cilantro is the name given to the little rounded seeds used in cooking.

When to plant: The seeds can be sown continuously indoors for a regular supply of fresh, tasty leaves. If grown outside, plant when there is no risk of frost (from May onwards normally). You can plant seed indoors then transplant it into the soil once the weather is warmer.

Best soil: Rich soil; add manure or homemade compost, with plenty of humus if available.

Best light: Full sun indoors; direct sunlight if outside.

Watering: If in the ground, water when the soil is dry at least once a week. When really dry, cilantro tries to go to seed so if you want seeds to save for your kitchen, that's perfect. Just make sure you keep planting new crops for leaves if you do this.

Plant next to: Tomatoes, chives, salads, marjoram.

Harvesting: Pick leaves regularly as needed. If you are growing for seeds, allow them to flower then let the plant die off and pick the seeds when they turn brown. When completely dry, store them in a glass jar for when you need them.

Cooking: A favorite ingredient in Mexican cooking, Italian dishes, and salads all over the world. Its fresh taste brings many dishes to life!

Problems: Often goes to seed but if that's why you are growing it, you won't mind! Keep planting new seeds to ensure you have a good supply of green cilantro leaves. Check if the leaves look wilted if cilantro is in pots, may need watering every day if hot.

Dill

Dill offers an attractive, feathery look for any flower bed with voluminous yellow flowers late in the summer, which turn to edible seeds. Dill leaves are long and very thin and look fabulous in fish dishes and cream sauces, adding a distinct flavor to cooking.

When to plant: Plant seeds in spring where you want them to grow. Dill does not take kindly to being re-planted and re-potted so or a little later when the soil is warm outside. Water them well.

Best soil: Dill requires well-drained soil and it grows up to 2 feet (60 cm) tall.

Best light: Full sun indoors; direct sunlight if outside.

Watering: Frequently, every day in hot weather or if the plant tries to go to seed.

Plant next to: Other flowering annual plants make good companions but not **fennel**. Fennel and Dill can cross-pollinate and the resulting plant will have an unpredictable taste. This plant can grow very tall and looks good at the back of a flower bed too, with other low flowering annuals placed in front.

Harvesting: Leaves can be harvested as required. The yellow flowers turn to seed heads. When they dry out and turn brown, you know when they are ready to pick. To collect, turn the seed head upside down into a paper bag and cut the stem so all the seeds fall into the bag.

Cooking: It is used in French cooking in sauces and fish dishes, particularly salmon. The dried herb leaves keep their flavor too, and you can hang them to dry in your kitchen. The seeds were traditionally used to make vinegar for pickling and they add a distinctive taste to cheese sauces.

Problems: Dill is usually happy to self-seed which may be a problem if you don't want too many plants. Pick the seed heads before they fall to avoid this. Some gardeners are not expecting the height to be so tall for an herb so seed it at the back of your flower bed, not the front.

Fennel

Fennel has an unmistakable smell – people seem to love it or hate it! Once established in a garden, it is there forever. It grows really tall and seeds hang on to the leaves all winter, enabling wind fertilization

When to plant: Plant the seeds in any patch where you want the herb, and more often than not, a plant will grow. Think carefully about its location. It will spread by seed dispersal and it grows taller than some adults in perfect conditions. Plant in April outside or slightly earlier indoors.

Best soil: Although it likes rich soil, fennel will grow anywhere! Fennel plants prefer well-drained soil.

Best light: Full sun indoors; direct sunlight if outside. Its height will shade smaller herbs so be careful where you plant it.

Watering:. Fennel loves frequent watering. However, it is native to windy, seaside cliffs so it can survive in conditions with infrequent rainfall. If fennel is in a pot, then water it weekly and avoid having the soil always moist.

Plant next to: Putting fennel at the back of a herb garden is perfect. You can plant fennel with other Mediterranean herbs like tarragon, thyme, rosemary, and even with tomatoes, chives, and cilantro, but not next to dill.

Harvesting: Pick leaves whenever you need them and eat as you walk, or add them to flavor soups and stews. You can dry fennel leaves too. Pick the seeds like dill, by placing a bag over the whole seed head and then catching the seeds as they fall.

Cooking: Try using fennel with oily fish, to use its distinctive taste. It is great steeped in a soup and removed before serving, along with a sprig of bay leaf and some thyme. The seed heads are excellent added as topping to homemade bread, bringing a taste of summer to the winter.

Problems: Fennel is a survivor and will spread like crazy so to avoid this, plant it at the back of a flower bed, cut the seed heads and save them for the kitchen and then use its stalks to support beans or peas..

Garlic

While you might not think of it as a herb, garlic is used all over the world and its health benefits, long-known to traditional knowledge have been confirmed by science..

When to plant: Garlic needs cold weather so plant in the fall, allow the winter to sharpen its taste, and gather the bulbs the following summer. Separate into individual cloves and plant each separately. Make sure the pointed end is up, as this will become the stalk. Sometimes you see a small root at the flatter end.

Best soil: Garlic needs good drainage and rich soil. Add manure if available, compost, and plenty of humus, such as leaf mold.

Best light: Best grown outside in pots or in a row in your garden. Bright summer sunshine is excellent.

Watering: Usually not necessary in winter except when first planted to establish the cloves in the ground. The rain normally does the work for you outside. Water weekly from spring onwards, especially if it is warm and sunny.

Plant next to: Some gardeners think planting peas and garlic together is a good idea as the peas fix nitrogen into the soil. Peas grow well in winter when the garlic is young and the soil will be enriched by the peas. However, peas can starve the garlic of nutrients at a time when they are establishing their first growth.

Harvesting: Garlic will tell you when it is ready to pick. The leaves turn brown and seem to die, allow a week or so for them to die off completely, then dig the garlic out. Store the bulbs by hanging them in a dry place.

Cooking: Used to make garlic bread, added to stews, soups, roasted, crushed into various Indian dishes, Chinese recipes, and all over the world.

Problems: Garlic has several diseases including root rot caused by extremely wet weather. There's nothing you can do apart from keeping an eye on the leaves. Plant them in rich soil with excellent drainage. The leaves also turn brown and appear dead when they are almost ready to harvest but this is just nature's way of telling you it is harvest time.

Lavender

This plant is used as a relaxant, lavender soap is used worldwide, and is added to clothes drawers and placed under pillows. Its delicious scent is a favorite with bees, so planting a few lavender plants will keep them very happy.

When to plant: Cuttings can be taken at any time, but best in spring or fall. More difficult to grow from seed, but if you do sow in early spring in pots. Give each plant space to expand because lavender will send shoots out in every direction. Most plants last at least 5 years but you will need to prune them regularly.

Best soil: Good drainage is essential. Lavender grows well on poor soil in native sites but if you give it some compost and enrich the soil with plenty of humus, your plants will thrive.

Best light: Loves full, direct sunlight outside.

Watering: Lavender does not need much water in the average garden. Once established, lavender does not need much unless it is an exceptionally hot, dry summer. Check the soil during those periods and water when it feels dry to the touch.

Plant next to: Plant it with other herbs in sunny spots and ensure that the taller lavender is at the back. In large pots, combine with nasturtiums, which add complementary colors to the silvery lavender leaves. The smell of lavender can confuse some garden flies, so try planting it next to anything attracting pests..

Harvesting: Cut your flowers in bloom in summer, which can be used to infuse oils with their scent. You will need to replace the flowers in the oil every week by adding new ones until the scent remains firmly embedded. Compost the flowers after use.

Cooking: Lavender leaves can be used to flavor meat dishes or as a strong taste in soups. It can be added to cake mixtures and batters too. The flowers are edible but you may need to balance their strong taste with citrus fruit like lime or lemon..

Problems: Lavender is usually trouble-free until it ages, after about 5 years. Stems can become long and woody and it is best to prune these to keep the plant in good shape. You can prune when you pick flowers, in the fall and the spring.

Lemon Balm

Also known as Bee Balm, this herb has a long history adding a citrus scent to various dishes, as well as making herbal teas. Fresh leaves can be added to salads to add a citrus taste in the summer sunshine.

When to plant: Plant seeds in spring but it is widely available in garden centers for those who want to plant direct!

Best soil: This herb grows well in most environments and rich soil is not essential. Plant it direct into a pot or your flower bed and give it some homemade compost or fresh soil. It does not need to be fertilized if the soil is reasonably fertile.

Best light: Lemon Balm is often grown in shade or semi-shade. Like mint, it is not a lover of really direct sunlight if outside. So a spot with some afternoon shade is ideal and the plant will thrive.

Watering: You don't need to water this plant too much outdoors. If it starts to flower, this is a sign that the plant may think winter is coming so you can cut the flowers off and extend its season a bit longer. Water when the soil around it seems very dry.

Plant next to: Lemon Balm spreads a lot so make sure neighbors are far away. Give it space but small herbs like parsley will grow well with it. Tomatoes, chives, cilantro, and marjoram are also good choices..

Harvesting: Leaves can be harvested when you need them in spring, summer, and fall. In winter it is fairly dormant so taking leaves then is hard on the herb. Cut leaves only when it's growing and allow it to rest for the winter.

Cooking: The leaves add a zing to cooked fruit and cakes and it is also added to stuffing mixtures mixed with breadcrumbs, where the flavor is infused in the poultry or meat is cooked with. Herbal tea made with lemon balm leaves and mint is a favorite tisane in many central European countries.

Problems: This herb does not stay in one place and its roots need to be divided after about 3 years, into independent plants. Some advice for a herb gardener with little space: plant this herb in a pot where you can restrict its growth.

Marjoram

Marjoram is occasionally mistaken for oregano. There are many varieties of this herb to try from annual plants which last only one growing season to bigger bush types like Pot Marjoram, which can survive for a few years

When to plant: Plant marjoram starters into the desired position in your garden in late spring. Sow seeds in March, then transplant outdoors when there is no danger of frost.

Best soil: Marjoram will tolerate soil that is not the richest; it is used to growing in the wild on dusty roadsides and cottage gardens. So give it some fresh compost but it will grow happily in many spots in the average garden without any problems.

Best light: Full sun outside is necessary for about 4 hours per day but marjoram tolerates some shade. It dries out very easily so some shade is perfect for this herb.

Watering: If in a pot, marjoram dries out very easily so water it at least weekly and check it during hot weather. Marjoram does fine with a regular splash, so you might have a look at it most days. If it needs water, it tends to flower, then go to seed.

Plant next to: Some herbs that prefer the same conditions are Lemon Balm, thyme, or mint. Its green leaves make an excellent background color for bright annual flowers like pansies and carnations, take advantage of the color and shape of its pretty leaves to add some artistic touches to the garden.

Harvesting: You can pick marjoram leaves as you need them in the growing season. Leaves can be picked and dried for winter use and you can also plant seeds late in the summer for a ready supply indoors throughout the winter.

Cooking: Marjoram is used to add its unique flavor to poultry or meat prior to cooking. Cooks spread a little oil on the meat and then crush the herb firmly into the skin so that the flavor will cook through. Add it to savory baking and the subtle taste will infuse the dish. Complements other herbs like thyme.

Problems: Frost is not a friend of your perennial marjoram so if you get cold winters either cover the plant well during a cold spot or better still, take it indoors. Annual marjoram will die back naturally at the end of the season.

Mint

Peppermint, spearmint, and many other varieties of mint can be grown. Mint is adored by bees and pollinators and there will be a hum around these plants when they are in bloom. Their flowers are attractive and the leaves are used to make teas.

When to plant: Either in spring or autumn, place a root in a container that restricts it from spreading. Mint is often described as invasive, so keep it in check in a pot. Cover with a generous layer of new topsoil each year and change the soil completely every 3 years.

Best soil: Mint uses up the goodness in soil quickly so if it starts to look unhealthy, add some compost to cheer it up! Good drainage is essential for mint too.

Best light: Mint enjoys the sun early morning and late afternoon but it prefers shade when the sun is at its hottest so make sure you provide it with some respite during the hottest parts of the summer.

Watering: As it lives in the shade during the hottest part of the day, most mint plants do well if watered by rainfall or once a week with a watering can.

Plant next to: Lemon Balm likes the same conditions but be careful with putting mint into the ground because it spreads so easily. If it is in a pot, then its fragrance is really pleasant in a seating area on a patio or its flower spikes look well next to other colorful annual flowers like nasturtiums or cosmos.

Harvesting: Pick leaves when you need them and you can also dry mint leaves for winter usage when the plant has died back. Mint dies back completely in winter so pick leaves before this happens.

Cooking: Mint sauce is a well-known recipe with lamb, and mint is also excellent in cool, refreshing summer drinks and mint ice cream is divine. Alcoholic drinks which contain mint include the cocktail favorite Crème de menthe and Mexican mojitos often come garnished with a mint leaf.

Problems: Mint is often the problem! It tends to take over entire gardens if permitted so keep it contained. It does have a Mint beetle which likes to lay its eggs on any mint but the plant usually survives. If you spot them, they are a very attractive metallic color and you can remove them or use a mixture of soap and water.

Oregano

This herb is frequently called wild marjoram and is often confused with sweet marjoram, which is very closely related to it. Common oregano is a member of the mint family and is used in Mediterranean cooking.

When to plant: Common oregano can be grown indoors in compost from March to May, and then transplanted out after the last frost. Heat is useful for germination so make sure your pot is in a warm place such if you don't have a heated mat to propagate seeds.

Best soil: Use compost for seeds, but oregano does not need very rich soil after germination. In the wild, it grows on Mediterranean clifftops where the soil is very sandy, so oregano will tolerate a wide variety of conditions as long as it is well-drained and not too wet! It prefers slightly acidic soil so adding some tea leaves or coffee grounds will help to create this over time.

Best light: This herb is used to the sunny slopes of cliff tops in southern Europe so give it a sunny position and a place where it remains warm. Full sun with some shelter is ideal..

Watering: Oregano prefers the soil to be dry, so it only needs a watering if the soil feels dry. If in a pot, oregano will need watering occasionally but do not allow the roots to be in wet, moist soil for too long.

Plant next to: Oregano's very delicate spikes of purple flowers look fabulous in any flower bed but you can also place oregano close to other herbs such as cilantro, parsley, or mint. It is perennial and will last many years in the same spot so allow it some space to expand too. It can grow up to 31 inches (80 cm).

Harvesting: Pick leaves as required in the growing period from spring through to the fall. You can add the leaves to olive oil, where the taste infuses the oil, depending on the cultivar you have chosen. Fresh leaves taste much stronger than the dried herb..

Cooking: The taste of your oregano will depend on the cultivar grown. The taste ranges from sweet in Europe, to bitter in some hybrids, to a spicier taste in Greece and Turkey, and a quite strong flavor in Latin America. Often eaten raw as a topping, but traditionally included in roasted dishes in Italian cooking.

Problems: Sometimes oregano just exhausts the soil it is in and needs to be moved. However, it is often best to completely change the site or start with a new plant. Experienced gardeners try to grow it from seed produced and have success.

Parsley

This herb comes as a garnish on salads, fish, and many dishes. Parsley sauce is chopped parsley added to a white sauce, which is used widely in the UK. Comes in both flat leaved parsley and moss curled varieties.

When to plant: Notoriously difficult to germinate, your parsley seeds need excellent care in order to grow. Germination will not take place in cold, wet soil so I advise using a warm dark place such as a heated gardening propagator or even your airing cupboard.

Best soil: Only the best for parsley! It likes rich soil with any extras such as leaf mold or homemade compost will ensure a long supply of green, tasty foliage.

Best light: Full sun indoors once the seeds germinate and then place plants in direct sunlight when you transplant them outside. If placed in the shade, it will not be as happy as in full sun. You can plant seeds late in the summer to take indoors for winter use.

Watering: Water frequently - every day in hot weather. The leaves wilt in really hot weather..

Plant next to: Parsley will mix happily with plants that like the same conditions. Tomatoes or cucumbers will give it a little shade when the sun is at its hottest, and it accompanies chives, cilantro, oregano, and marjoram well too.

Harvesting: Pick as needed for fresh use, dried parsley is not ideal. Some cooks swear by dipping a few sprigs of parsley into boiling water for 1-2 minutes, then placing it to dry in the oven for a few minutes. As soon as it cools, place it in a spice jar to use in winter (or a late summer sowing to take some fresh parsley indoors for the winter).

Cooking: Eat fresh in summer salads, use as a garnish on fish, as a topping for scrambled eggs, and in white for potatoes. Parsley is one of the herbs in the French *Fines Herbes* and is often added as a last-minute topping on soups and stews.

Problems: The main difficulty is germination but once established, parsley is usually trouble-free. Slugs and snails are partial to the young leaves so keep your eyes peeled. You also need to pick regularly to stop it from going to seed. If flowers appear, cut them off to stop the plant from going to seed.

Rosemary

Rosemary for remembrance, because the scent of this herb will remain even in a dried sprig months later. Rosemary needs plenty of space, as this perennial herb will expand its branches and delight you with sky blue flowers in spring.

When to plant: You can sow seeds in April or May but they take quite a while to germinate. It might be better to buy a small plant and position it in a warm spot where it will thrive. Rosemary can tolerate a cold winter but it likes a sheltered spot. Frost may kill off the tips of an established plant but new shoots will emerge when the weather warms up.

Best soil: Rosemary grows wild on French and Italian coastlines. To imitate this, plant it in sandy, well-drained soil which does not retain excess moisture. A handful of compost won't go amiss every spring and fall but Rosemary grows happily in fairly poor soil.

Best light: Full sun is best. Provide heat and some shelter from winter weather by planting it next to a south-facing wall or near other shrubs which will protect it from winter frost.

Watering: As a cliff plant, Rosemary does not need to be watered once it is established. Allow rainfall to do that job for you! For the newly planted Rosemary plant, water it well and then keep an eye on it for a few months, giving it only the occasional watering.

Plant next to: Rosemary needs space to reach its full height and spread as an herb; however, it also needs shelter from very cold weather so planting it close to rose bushes and other garden shrubs often helps. Frost will kill off the growing tips but it shouldn't damage the roots so don't worry too much.

Harvesting: Pick the fresh leaves or a whole sprig to add flavor to stews, casseroles, and cooked dishes. Pick sprigs to dry indoors and hang them in clothes cupboards, or areas where you need a fresh smell, and then use the dried leaves as required throughout the winter.

Cooking: Rosemary leaves leave a scent on your hands long after cutting so use sparingly; the flavor is very strong. Usually, cooks add a sprig of Rosemary and remove it before serving. Rosemary accompanies lamb, pork, and veal in Mediterranean recipes and it adds depth to vegetarian meals.

Problems: Winter frost or snow appears to kill off the growing tips of Rosemary but it usually survives. If you are worried, then cover the plant with a cloth or bubble wrap for the cold period.

Sage

Sage looks elegant at all times of the year. The leaves have an unusual texture and the herb comes in various shades and colors from dark olive-green to gray, an attractive addition to any garden.

When to plant: Try not to plant sage into cold ground; spring is ideal once the last frosts have passed. Choose a sunny site and make sure you do not have other plants very close. Apart from strawberries and borage, sage emits a chemical signal to other plants which deters their growth.

Best soil: If planting into the ground, add compost and plenty of humus, which will decompose slowly and add essential nutrients. Sage will grow for many years so start the ground well. Do not expect sage to stay small – it can reach as high as 3 feet (91.5 cm) tall and expands in all directions.

Best light: Full sun is essential for sage to reach its growth potential. It will dominate after 2 years so do not plant delicate plants next to it.

Watering: Sage enjoys natural rainfall, don't bother watering sage unless you have just planted it. Water it weekly in its first few months but after that, let the rain do the work. Check the soil and make sure it is dry before watering.

Plant next to: Choose robust geraniums or annuals until a new sage plant reaches its full height. After that, surround it with strawberries and borage, maybe chives or parsley but not too close. Sage tends to kill off other plants that grow too close.

Harvesting: A little sage goes a long way. Pick leaves fresh before the plant has flowered, which is usually June or July.

Cooking: Sage is well known for the flavor it adds to stuffing for poultry and meat on festive occasions and modern bread makers have made it popular as a flavor too. It is a very strong herb and may overwhelm other herbs. Some cheesemakers use a little sage too and other uses (sparingly) are in soups, stews, and slow-cooked dishes where the herb can release its goodness slowly.

Problems: Sage can overwhelm other plants close to it. So if you have a favorite plant, think twice before adding a sage plant close by. As it grows, it gets woody and you will need to prune it hard every July after it flowers.

Savory (Summer)

Savory comes as a winter and summer herb, and summer savory tastes like a mixture of thyme, sage, and rosemary.

When to plant: Like its winter relative, this herb is best planted in Spring (April) and can be treated as an annual, so plant new seeds each year. Cover seeds with a thin layer of compost and watch it climb to over 1 foot (30 cm) tall

Best soil: The soil needs to have good drainage and to be light, not a clay type. Ensure you add some compost and if your soil is very thick, maybe add some sand and gravel to thin it a little.

Best light: Full sun is best in a new position each year.

Watering: As this herb likes good drainage you do not need to water very frequently. When it's very dry weather, feel the soil and if it's really parched give it a good soaking. When it flowers, it likes some water too so when you spot the buds, get your watering can out.

Plant next to: This is an annual herb so you can happily plant it next to any herb that likes similar soil and watering. If space is tight, then parsley, chives, cilantro, and marjoram are all good companions although some of these prefer the soil a bit richer.

Harvesting: You need to pick leaves before the plant flowers when the herb is about 1 foot (30 cm) high. After you've enjoyed the flowers, cut the whole plant back and then it should produce a second crop of leaves. Pick these until your winter savory appears!

Cooking: Savory can be used like thyme or rosemary in most dishes. It adds depth to the flavor and the silvery gray leaves emit a gorgeous scent when cut in the kitchen. Add them to egg dishes, they can go in salads and they are an extra taste to experiment with when cooking summer dishes.

Problems: When seeds are first planted, keep an eye out for slugs and snails which will gobble them up. You can grow them in a pot and transplant them, but these seeds are not fond of disturbance.

Savory (Winter)

Savory comes as a winter and summer herb, and winter savory offers the cook an herb they can pick when very little is in season.

When to plant: Winter savory is an evergreen plant, which provides leaves in the depth of winter like sage and thyme. For this reason alone, it is worth giving it a try! Plant it in your soil in April and make sure you trim it back in spring. It then goes quite dormant until the weather cools down and summer savory takes over

Best soil: Light soil with good drainage will suit winter savory very well. It is a low, ground-hugging herb that enjoys full sun when few other plants are there to compete. It grows in spikes, with leaves shooting out to each side which you can pick for salads, omelets, and winter poached eggs..

Best light: Full sun outdoors. Try to make sure bigger shrubs do not shade it or the foliage will be thin.

Watering: Frequently every day in hot water or it goes to seed.

Plant next to: Winter savory has fresh, new leaves from early fall and many other plants are dying back at this time so the usual plants to accompany this herb are winter flowering bulbs such as snowdrops, grape hyacinths, and later on, daffodils. The problem with these is that they tend to spread through an area and they may overwhelm your winter savory. My advice is to either give this herb its own, deep pot and have a label on it to remind you or you that you place a mulch on top of it to mark its position and then plant around it in the summer.

Harvesting: Pick leaves frequently for fresh use in the winter and spring months. Then ensure that you cut the herb back in late spring to allow it to rest before it appears again the following winter.

Cooking: Savory is traditionally used to season broad bean and lentil soup. Broad beans are ready to pick in late March, early April so herbs may still be growing fresh leaves. You can also use winter savory for fresh green garnishes to egg dishes and to accompany any green salads.

Problems: You may think your winter savory has completely died when the hot, midsummer sun is shining in your garden but it is just taking a rest! Otherwise, its leaves are munched by slugs and snails but it is usually not bothered by pests in the cold season.

Tarragon

There is no taste quite like tarragon! This herb is delicate with a hint of licorice. Two types of tarragon are available; French and Russian.

When to plant: You cannot plant French tarragon from seed. Normally it spreads through its rhizome root system and the seeds rarely grow into new viable plants. Buy a starter plant instead, but it will not tolerate frost and is quite difficult to grow. The Russian variety can be planted in spring indoors and then planted outdoors when the ground is warm. It is tolerant of frost once established, and is much less picky in general.

Best soil: French tarragon likes rich soil which drains well. Russian tarragon will grow happily in semi-shade in less fertile soil, which its choosier French cousin will not.

Best light: French tarragon loves being indoors in full sun. It needs to be indoors the minute the fall arrives because a frost will kill it immediately. Outdoors, give French tarragon a sunny position and it will grow the whole summer season. Russian tarragon enjoys bright sunlight if outside, but as long as it has 4 hours per day, this herb will continue to thrive..

Watering: In pots, both of these herbs need frequent watering but neither likes roots that sit in wet soil.

Plant next to: French tarragon does not take up a lot of space. Annual flowers and herbs like parsley are excellent but do not crowd it by planting it next to rosemary or other taller plants. You will need to dig it up carefully to take it indoors for winter so if you keep it in a pot, you can do this easily.

Russian tarragon needs less fertile soil, and foxgloves love the shade and similar conditions so this could be a good choice.

Harvesting: For drying, French tarragon is the better to use because the Russian variety tends to lose scent as it dries. Both herbs are rich in vitamin A and C so eat them fresh when you can.

Cooking: Tarragon is added to seafood, salads, sauces, flavored butter to melt onto poultry, as well as in sweet rice dishes and desserts. Both varieties work well with vanilla pods and sometimes you will find this served in French ice cream or sweet sauces. Tarragon vinegar is a favorite for salads and either herb can be used.

Russian tarragon stalks can be cooked fresh when they are young, similar to bamboo shoots and asparagus. It is a more vigorous plant so you can pick more leaves and add them to salads, giving them an unusual twist.

Thyme

Thyme is a perennial evergreen herb, with dainty little pink flowers, which tends to creep along dry areas in impoverished soils. Plant it somewhere to enjoy the scent of the leaves and the herb's pretty blooms. You can pick its leaves all year round.

When to plant: You can plant the seed in late spring when the ground has warmed up, but most growers buy a plant instead. Thyme grows quite leggy with straggling branches over time. Plant it deep and make sure the soil has good drainage as thyme hates wet feet! Divide plants every 3 years and replant them separately.

Best soil: Thyme will thrive in poor soil; this herb is a great survivor. Give it a thin layer of compost (around the stem) in the spring, to encourage it to grow big and strong. Leaf mold will add humus and it seems to appreciate it. In the summer, make a mulch with grass cuttings which decompose slowly and reduce loss of moisture.

Best light: Full sun indoors or outdoors. Thyme thrives with lots of sunshine.

Watering: Infrequently. Most thyme plants survive very hot temperatures with little rainfall in their native Mediterranean environments so it is not necessary to water your thyme plant much. In a particularly dry period, check its soil and water if it feels really parched..

Plant next to: Any Mediterranean herb (chives, rosemary, cilantro, parsley). Thyme will not grow much higher than 1 foot (about 30 cm) so place it at the front of plants that grow taller. This makes it easier to pick leaves too.

Harvesting: Pick thyme leaves fresh throughout the year as you need them. This herb survives the winter and you can keep cutting to add flavor to cooking. A great herb for climates where little else can be picked fresh.

.**Cooking:** Thyme often accompanies parsley in bread, and is often added to fish because it is a subtle taste that does not overwhelm delicate flavors. It adds flavor to soups like squash and pumpkin and can be added to pastry as a topping. Some cooks add it to desserts like lemon and thyme cake because the taste is accentuated by sugar and slow cooking releases the flavor.

Problems: Thyme gets very leggy if left unpruned. Most thyme plants use up the nutrients for the soil they are in after about 3 years so it is a good idea to divide the roots and re-plant them.

Chapter 4
How to Sow, Propagate and Divide Herbs

TO HAVE A STEADY SUPPLY OF FRESH HERBS IS VERY EASY IN summer and many herbs only last for just one season. However, some herbs can have a much longer life if divided or cut to make new plants. This chapter examines best practices for sowing herbs from seed and how to propagate new herbs so that you can have a steady supply year-round.

All seeds require soil, water, and heat to germinate. Use sterilized soil to start seeds off so you know there are no diseases, pests, or weeds present. Seeds take different times to begin life – see the soil requirements for each herb in Chapter 3.

Here are the ideal conditions for germinating seeds:

Temperature. Herbs, like most plants, have a minimum and optimum temperature to ensure they germinate. In the wild, this is so that the plant seed will not try to start growing until the temperature feels like spring or until the perfect growing conditions for the seed to be viable exist. This is approximately 18 or 19 degrees Celsius for most herbs (64 to 68 degrees Fahrenheit) but can be a slightly higher 20 to 23 Celsius (68 to 73 degrees

Fahrenheit) for tomatoes, chili peppers, and cucumbers, which may accompany your herbs. Buying a heated propagation mat will be very useful in a climate with cold winters.

Water the pot when you plant the seed and then wait a bit. The goal here is to keep the soil just moist. Once the seeds are established, follow the watering guidelines for each herb in Chapter 3. An optional trick is to leave your seeds in a bowl of warm water until you can see them start to sprout and then transfer them to the soil.

Light is another factor. Celery, for example, needs light to germinate, so you should just place the seeds on top of the compost and water them in. As soon as any of your herb seeds show some green growth, they will need light to photosynthesize. For early sowings in spring, you may need some help from artificial light to help your herb seedlings to thrive because light levels tend to be very low before the beginning of spring.

Choosing your Seeds

Not all seeds are the same, so choose your seeds carefully. Some seeds are called F1, which means they have been altered to make them resistant to disease or produce more fruit. These can be useful for plants that tend to become diseased (cabbage family, potatoes, etc.) or if you want to grow more productive crops (squash). However, the taste is another issue and for me, buying organic seed usually guarantees that my crops get the best possible start.

Starting your Seeds

A good trick for seeds that are difficult to get going (like parsley) is to give them a few hours in water to soften them up. You can place several seeds in a pot of compost, water them, then cover them up with a thin layer of soil. Then cover the whole seed pot with a transparent plastic bag to trap moisture. Use any plastic you have handy from shopping bags or food wrap; this will conserve moisture, retain heat better, and can be removed as soon as your seedlings show. Next, supply some heat! An airing cupboard is superb for this but only for one or two pots at a time! Some gardeners prefer to use a heated propagation mat, which supplies heat for many pots simultaneously and can keep seedlings at a steady temperature. Until seeds have germinated, they don't need light in general apart from celery and some salads.

Check each day for new seedlings, and if the soil feels dry, water the pot every 2 to 3 days. As soon as the seedlings appear, remove the plastic cover and move them into the light in a protected environment. For example, a sunny windowsill indoors in spring is perfect but be careful with drafts when the nighttime temperature falls. As the days get warmer, place the seedlings outdoors to harden them off; this is a time outside in the sunshine to help them get used to being outdoors, but take them back in at night away from pests and from dangerous drops in temperature.

Thinning out

This is the process of separating the seedlings and keeping only the strongest ones. It is not such a big issue with herbs, but when growing basil, cilantro, and salad crops, I grow plenty of herb seeds and then space them into the final growing spot. I usually plant them all because this allows for some spoilage by slugs and snails but usually ensures that many plants will survive.

It is essential to check how tall and wide your final herb will reach. For example, if you grow a tomato next to your basil, chives, and cilantro, you need to remember that some tomato varieties can reach over 2 feet tall and spread to at least 2 feet wide. A tiny tomato in a pot gives you no indication of the maximum height it can reach, so check the seed packet, stake the tomato before you add the plant to the soil, and allow it some space away from its herb neighbors. Your basil will be completely shaded unless you think about this before you dig in the companion tomato, and you already know that basil likes the sun. With herbs that will grow much bushier like sage, allow the herb enough space to grow into its final size.

Potting on

When your herb seedlings start to look cramped, their roots begin to show at the base of the pot, and the sunny weather has arrived, it is time to pot your herbs on. This means either giving them a bigger pot or planting them directly into the soil in the ground or a planter bed. First, check the soil needs for your particular herb in Chapter 3. Some herbs do not need rich soil, and some prefer it. When sowing seeds directly into the soil, make sure you dig a hole big enough for the root ball of your herb (only slightly larger than the root ball size), that the soil is crumbly, and that you water them in well.

Propagation: making more plants

Why should you do it?

1. Cost – you can make new, free plants. If your neighbors have a plant you like, just ask them for a cutting!
2. Some herbs do not grow from seed (e.g., French tarragon). Making new plants will make welcome gifts for family and friends.
3. All herbs eventually get old, so this allows you to replace your favorites with new vigorous ones just like their parent.

The Essesntial Herb Gardening Handbook

4. Hormone rooting powder or gel makes it a straightforward process. However, commercial ones are very reliable, and there are some natural alternatives in the Tips below.

The main ways to propagate your herbs

Take stem cuttings

Cut a small part of a healthy secondary stem approximately 3-6 inches (8-15 cm) long off of the plant. Make your cut close to the main stem if possible. Ensure there are no flower buds on the stem piece you remove because the herb will try to flower, not root. Next, remove the leaves at the end of the stem. Now you can either root the stem in water or plant it directly into the soil.

Place the stem(s) in a jar of water and allow it to sit in a shady area for a few weeks. Roots should start to grow, and as soon as you see a robust root system, you can pot this new plant in the soil. Dip the end of the stem into hormone rooting powder to help the process along (see natural alternatives below). Make a hole for the cutting in a pot of sterilized compost and ease the soil around the new root. Water it generously to assist the plant in stabilizing.

Woody stems from herbs like rosemary and sage will take longer to root, so be patient. Rooting is easier with some help from either a commercial hormone rooting powder or a natural one. Water it well every 3 to 4 days and place it in a sunny location. Check the soil daily and watch for any new leaves forming. If they start growing, your plant is ready to go.

This works for: bay, basil, lavender, oregano, sage, rosemary, tarragon, thyme.

TIPS: A natural hormone rooting powder is the gel from Aloe

Vera if you have a plant. Other alternatives used by gardeners worldwide include cinnamon, turmeric, honey, willow tea, comfrey tea, and even cow dung! Run the cut end of the stem over the gel and then place the stem directly in the soil.

Take root cuttings

This is also known as plant division. Many herbs become very overgrown over time, and my advice is to pick herb leaves frequently as a natural pruning process. After all, you grew them for a reason, don't forget to use them! Herbs like mint quickly outgrow any pot they live in, and every three years or so, you need to divide the roots and re-pot to keep the plant healthy. Dig up the whole herb carefully, and then use a spade or knife to cut sections of the herb off with stem, leaves, and roots intact. If you grow this division in soil, it will usually make a brand new plant.

This works for chives, mint, oregano, Lemon Balm, thyme, winter savory.

TIPS: Check the herb at the end of the season and decide if it needs division. Are there very woody branches? Does it hang over the edge of the pot? If so, you can prune it back vigorously or divide the roots

OTHER PLANTS REPRODUCE BY GROWING SMALL PLANTLETS (Spider plant and Aloe vera), or they self-seed by throwing ripe seeds into the soil in areas at a distance from the mother herb.

This is true for dill, fennel, parsley, and Russian tarragon.

TIPS: If your herb is becoming invasive, make sure to remove seed heads just after flowering.

Chapter 5
Soil Improvement and Companion Planting

THIS CHAPTER WILL EXAMINE WAYS TO IMPROVE YOUR SOIL USING composting and other free methods of recycling waste to create richer soil for all your plants and wildlife in general. Companion planting means using Mother Nature to pair plants up that help each other in some way. Finally, we will look at what can go wrong with your herbs in Chapter 7 and include crop rotation.

Your herbs may be the only crop you want to grow. However, it is worth knowing how to improve your soil if you plan on growing herbs for more than one season. Soil is food for your herbs, and the microscopic creatures that inhabit our soil can create their own thriving ecosystem, even in a pot on your windowsill. So let's look at some easy ways to ensure that your soil is healthy and some ways to improve it so that it can support your herbs (and plants) for years to come.

Ways to improve your soil for your herbs

If you buy a bag of compost in the garden center, it will undoubtedly have enough nutrients to feed your herbs for one growing season. However, if you dig into your soil outdoors, you should expect to see some wildlife! If you find earthworms, they are aerating the soil as they tunnel through it, and you will often see centipedes scurrying back under cover. Worms deposit their waste, which adds to soil fertility, and there may be other creatures alive in a handful of soil, this is a living substance.

Soil gets quickly depleted if one type of plant keeps extracting all the goodness so, in order to continue to grow healthy plants and herbs, you need to add a top layer to pots or herbs in the ground. For herbs, a soil pH of about 6.8 is usually recommended, and soil should be crumbly like the texture of bread crumbs. However, individual herbs may have preferences, so check Chapter 3 when you are planting for detailed information.

To test what type of soil you have in the ground, dig a hole at least 1 foot (approximately 30 cm) deep and then pour a whole watering can of water into it. Watch how the water drains away. If it's straight through, you probably have sandy soil. If the water still has not drained away 24 hours later, you may have clay soil. The ideal soil is loam – see more below.

Sandy soil is found near the ocean, and it is not as full of nutrients as other soils, mainly because these drain away every time it rains. It can be dug relatively easily has excellent drainage, but conversely, this means goodness is leached out of the soil. To counteract this, add some sawdust, well-rotted manure, and compost to enrich it for hungry vegetables. Sandy soil is perfect for some herbs because it is the norm in their native environments, so check the details of your particular herb in Chapter 3.

Loam soil (the best soil!) has a texture like crumbs; you can dig it easily when it is dry, it drains well, and usually has high fertility. It retains moisture well but not to the extent that rainfall gathers in puddles on the top of the soil when it rains. If that happens, you probably have clay soil.

Clay soil sticks together like modeling clay. Imagine this around a plant's roots. It may cause the ground to get waterlogged, so if your soil has a lot of clay, it is good to add other ingredients to help make it looser. For example, some sand can be added, and some homemade compost is another good idea. Both of these will add other nutrients and allow for better drainage.

Before you plant any herbs, check for the exact conditions they like in Chapter 3. Then use the ways below to improve fertility generally for soil which grows crops year after year.

HERE ARE EIGHT EASY WAYS YOU CAN IMPROVE YOUR SOIL YEAR on year.

1. Use well-rotted manure: Manure adds richness and nutrients to any garden, and if you cannot find a local farmer or stable to supply it, buy a bag from a supplier or garden center. If you have any friends who have chickens, a bucket full of soil from wherever they run is equally good to increase the quality of your soil. Dig it in well, and it needs to be well-rotted. Manure is really useful to feed hungry crops like tomatoes, and if you are planting basil right next door, both crops will benefit from a bucket full of manure. Plant cilantro, chives, and lettuce in the same bed next to the tomatoes; all of these plants will guzzle up the manure to make sumptuous tomatoes and lots of fantastic herb foliage and green leaves to add to salads.

2. Compost your waste: This recycling of green waste brings many nutrients into the soil and stops it from going to a landfill. I cannot recommend this enough. Even a small worm composter is helpful if you only have a small space. If you have soil and a backyard, buy a big plastic composting bin with a top lid to place material in easily and a door below to extract the finished product. Start with a layer of twigs or cardboard on the soil. Then empty your tea bags, coffee grounds, potato peelings, apple cores, orange peels, and anything that has ever grown in there. Composting is a method of reducing your environmental waste by decomposing it into planting material in as little as six months. It can take longer, but there are guides to the best methods available, and your local authority is a good start.

For simple composting, you need to alternate layers with green waste like vegetable peelings, then add a second layer of paper or wood waste from garden twigs, leaves, etc. Paper waste like newspapers, envelopes, and household bills can also be added but tear them into tiny pieces to aid in decomposition. Grass lawn cuttings, twigs chopped finely, any skin or peels from fruit or vegetables, and the dust from the vacuum bag waste is fine in there. Crush eggshells and these will add keratin and calcium.

DO NOT ADD cooked meat, fish or dairy products, or pet litter trays for fear of attracting rodents or risk of cross-infection. Instead, you can make a DIY composting area by using pallets or old wooden planks and then using an old carpet or cardboard to cover up the whole area.

3. Mulches: Gardeners often speak about adding a layer of mulch to the top of a plant pot or flower bed. This is simply spreading a layer of material on the topsoil such as composted wood chips, freshly cut lawn mowings, straw, hay, comfrey leaves, leaf mold (see below), or green manure material (such as ryegrass and corn salad).

You can do the same with your pots. Just add a layer on the top and water it in. The idea is often to block weeds with this layer and retain moisture in very hot weather. Wood chips should be used with care, as some gardeners complain that they deplete the soil underneath. However, they are great for use on walkways or paths between your herb garden pots or growing beds.

4. Seaweed: This is a method used by Irish farmers for centuries, and if you live close to the sea, this is a free resource. You can buy seaweed liquid feed in any garden center! Simply gather some seaweed and spread it on the top of the soil at the end of the growing season in winter or early in spring. This will give it time to decompose, and it not only adds goodness to the soil but also helps as a technique for water retention. Make sure you keep it away from the stems of the plants you want to grow though – keep it at the edges of the border. A layer of seaweed keeps the soil moist at ground level. If you find it difficult to weed, this layer reduces weeding because other plants find it difficult to survive with a blanket of salty, decomposing seaweed. It is a tried and tested method to deter slugs and other pests. In addition, it enriches the soil and can give lethargic plants a boost. Finally, it helps lighten dense soil, and it's free! Some gardeners are not so keen on the smell of seaweed, but if, like me, you love the ocean smells, just try it.

5. Ash: Do you burn logs in winter to keep warm, and maybe you have access to ash from bonfires during the year? Ash is the remains of wood, and it is high in nutrients which can raise fertility. Just add a layer to the topsoil. When you add it to either pots or soil, make sure you mix it in equal parts with compost because otherwise, it can change the pH of the soil very quickly, and the life forms within the soil may not be entirely happy with a layer of ash thrown all over them. Using compost and ash together provides the nutrients you can water in so that the combined goodness soaks into the soil below.

6. Leaf mold: If you ever have to sweep up garden leaves, this will make that job more manageable. Make some holes in a big plastic bag and then add the leaves and simply leave them until the spring. The holes will allow air to circulate, and the leaves will decompose naturally. Come springtime, have a look and there will be a crumbly, dry leaf textured mixture that adds extra humus to the soil. You will probably find that creatures have found this safe, warm place (like earthworms and caterpillars) so when you empty the bag, remove these to a safer place. Add it to seed mixes with compost, and you can also dig it into any planter box with herbs in it.

7. Green manures: are seeds that are sown either in winter or spring when land lies fallow for a season or two. Sowing these crops fixes nitrogen into the soil and makes it available for the next crop you plant – your herbs. Sow the seeds in the pot the winter before you plant herbs and let the green manure crop grow freely until the spring. Then turn the whole plant upside down in the pot, which will become nutrients for your hungry herbs. Examples of green manures are clover, phacelia, Hungarian ryegrass. If you ask more experienced gardeners or your local seed supplier, they may know others more suitable for your local climate and soil.

8. Crop rotation: Over the centuries, gardeners have noticed that soil cannot support the same crop in the same soil every year. In agricultural terms, this is known as monoculture, and it makes crops more liable to infestation by pests and disease. To counteract this, crop rotation is a system that rotates the crop in the same area every 3-4 years.

Companion planting for herbs

On the next page, we will look at various herbs which grow well (or poorly) with other plants. Some gardeners use herbicides, pesticides, and barrier methods to remove pests and most herbs

The Essesntial Herb Gardening Handbook

have aromatic scents, which are helpful. You may be able to avoid a lot of the damage caused by pests merely by planting a good neighbor, so let's walk ourselves through this!

Herb	Possible Companion	Reason
Basil	Asparagus, tomatoes, and parsley	Asparagus root fly and aphids hate the smell of basil.
Celery	Lettuce and salad crops	Short growing season – no competition and they have similar soil is required. Not parsnips, turnips, or carrots
Chives	Carrots, parsley, marjoram, tarragon	They repel aphids and the smell of chives is hated by carrot root flies and other pests
Dill	Coriander	Beneficial insects, and dill is taller and shades it. Attracts insects away from coriander.
Fennel	Broad beans	Ladybugs love fennel flowers and will eat blackfly on broad beans. Not dill or cilantro, cross breeds with dill and crowds out cilantro.
Garlic	Asparagus	The strong smell keeps pests away, so can be helpful near any vegetables.
Lemon Balm	Mint – but keep it in a pot	Similar growing conditions. Both attract beneficial insects.
Marjoram	See chives	Nasturtiums work well with this herb too and attract aphids away from it.
Mint	Shade-loving plants like Lemon Balm	Attracts beneficial insects, but will crowd out most other plants.
Oregano	Other Mediterranean herbs	Similar soil and watering (keep soil dry).
Parsley	See basil	Grows well in rich soil, more foliage if well-watered.
Rosemary	Bay leaf	Deters pests. Great pollinator flowers and strong scent.
Summer savory	Onions	Next to onions, they say it makes onions sweeter. Attracts pollinators.
Winter savory	Lavender or thyme	
Sage	Strawberries and borage, or cabbages and carrots	Its strong smell deters pests from visiting berries, cabbages, and carrots. Also deters growth in some plants, so give it some
Tarragon	Dill and lavender	They attract pollinators. Remember to take indoors in winter.
Thyme	Mediterranean herbs – rosemary	Same soil needs and both attract pollinators

Chapter 6
History and Basic Techniques

This chapter will examine how herbs were used in times gone by, and provide some basic techniques for using herbs. For example, cottage gardens were used to provide herbs to contemporary doctors in the Middle Ages, and herbs have been used worldwide to soothe colds, improve appetite, cure headaches, and reduce fever. In addition, monastery gardens often produced fine wines and spirits for monarchs, and some of these were infused with herbs. Read on for a whistle-stop tour of herbs in history and how you can use that knowledge today to make your own herb oils, in cooking, and to replace various household products.

Herbs in history

When you think of a time without refrigeration or freezing, herbs were used dried, preserved in oil, and as a way to cover up the smell of food that may have passed its sell-by date. Midwives and mothers widely recognized that certain herbs provided relief from pain, fever, and other symptoms. Physicians often had a patch in the cottage garden for herbs believed to have medicinal benefits, even if these cannot be proven today. At a time when no pharmaceutical drugs were available, herbs were used as substitutes for medicine. Digitalis, for example, extracted from foxglove flowers, is still utilized for heart conditions. While this book does not recommend the exclusive use of herbs, chat to your doctor about using them alongside your medicine. For each herb, I have added ways it was used in the past and ways you can use it now. Have fun!

Drying herb leaves for winter use, making herb oil, and making teas from fresh leaves are simple ways to benefit from your homegrown herbs. In the days before freezers, kitchens would dry lots of herbs for use in colder weather when the fresh herb was unavailable; this makes for delightful smells in the area where you hang them to dry. Children love helping with this activity, and if you give them a long piece of string, they can help by tying individual herbs together as they become ready for picking. Alcohol and oil-infused herbs preserved the scent and the goodness well, and you can find several recommendations below for the best herbs to do this. Herb oils have a long history in usage and are referred to in ancient Egyptian texts and medical writings from India, Babylon, the Middle East, and China. Every culture prized certain herbs for specific characteristics, and a trip to your local aromatherapist can enlighten you on their usage today.

Read on for a discussion of each herb below, along with a basic recipe or technique. Make sure you experiment and get creative with these basics, and develop your own herb creations!

Basil

is an essential ingredient of Italian cooking in salads, pizzas, and sauces. Pesto sauce is a firm favorite in many households. Here is a recipe to make your own.

You will need:

- a cup or a good handful of fresh basil leaves
- 2-3 tablespoons of pine nuts
- at least half a cup of olive oil
- 2-3 cloves of garlic
- half a cup of grated Parmesan cheese
- freshly ground black pepper, and
- a pinch of sea salt

Method:

To make a smooth sauce, you need to liquefy the basil leaves in a food processor or blender. Next, remove the skins of the garlic and chop the garlic into smaller pieces. Then mix all the ingredients except the olive oil in a bowl. You can add these ingredients to the bowl of a food processor to arrive at a smooth paste. Next, add small amounts of the olive oil, and continue stirring this in. It will gradually become absorbed, and you can keep adding the oil until you get to whatever consistency you prefer. This will store in the fridge for a week, and then you can make another fresh batch.

Bay leaf

is grown as a shrub or tree, and besides its use in cooking, it can also be added to bottles of herb oil to add its unique flavor over time. Bay leaves must be dried before you use them. So prune several branches of your bay and then hang them in a shady spot for several weeks – 2-4 is ideal. This will infuse the air where you store them, and I thoroughly recommend allowing them to hang for the whole winter and just picking them when you need them!

Remember that botulism is sometimes a problem for herbs that you add to oil, so check all your herb leaves carefully for pests and remove them first. Do not use damaged leaves. Some gardeners recommend using a citric acid wash for herbs before adding them to oil. Once added, you need to seal the bottle, so use screw top lids or a cork but make sure it remains closed. When in use, just sniff the bottle. Anything that smells good is usually an indication that everything is perfect for use.

You will need:

A bottle of olive oil; I recommend virgin olive oil or whatever oil is produced closest to you for a more sustainable version. Check the provenance of your closest suppliers and purchase locally if possible. If you have a decorative empty wine bottle, this is a great way to use it!

Method:

Ensure the bottle is completely clean by sterilizing it or washing it well in a bowl of boiling water, then dry it in an oven at low heat. Next, fill half of the bottle with oil and add one or two bay leaves on a twig stem. You can include other herbs such as a sprig of thyme, some tarragon, and rosemary, which also grow on twigs but make sure there are not too many flavors, or they will compete! Then fill the bottle up to the top and seal it.

Make sure it looks aesthetically pleasing and allow the bottle to sit in a shady place, without direct sunlight for 2-3 weeks, by which time the oil will be infused with flavor.

This makes a fabulous salad dressing oil, and it looks terrific sitting on the dinner table too. How about making a perfect, homemade gift? Make a fresh bottle about a month before the festive season, add a red ribbon bow, and it is ideal for Christmas presents.

CELERY

has water-filled celery stems which are fantastic if added to homemade juices, adding an unexpected zing to the flavor. It is a fresh taste all on its own, and you can combine it with apples for a sweeter taste.

Celery seed can be saved as it arrives and then used as a seasoning like salt) or made into tea. Celery seed tea is said to be useful for the elimination of toxins from the body but just once a day. Check with your medical professional if in doubt. Parsley tea is also recommended for this, but please seek medical advice, and if you are taking medication, check with your physician first.

Chives

are not as good dried as they are fresh, but you can grow spring onions all year round for a similar flavor. I love chive butter when these delicious greens are in season.

You will need:

- 200g of butter
- a handful of chives
- some salt and pepper, and
- a handful of parsley is also recommended.

You can increase quantities if you have more guests.

Method:

Allow the butter to soften slightly at room temperature for half an hour before use. Then, place it in a bowl. Chop your chives finely to release that gorgeous, oniony flavor, and then mix them into the butter. You can simmer in a pan at a low temperature on the stove for a few minutes to help the chive flavor absorb into the butter.

Use melted onto fish dishes and also on baked potatoes. Very fattening but delicious!

CILANTRO

is known as coriander in the UK, but in the US and Canada, cilantro is the leaf and coriander is the seed. Cilantro leaf is now a favorite for infusion in gins and is widely available commercially. Cilantro's sweet taste adds an unusual flavor to desserts like rice puddings if you can add it at low heat, allowing the herb to infuse. However, coriander seed is essential for making your own curry mixture so let's get started!

You will need:

- 1 tablespoon each of coriander
- fenugreek and cumin seeds
- a small piece of grated ginger
- a teaspoon of turmeric
- some chili to suit your taste.

You also need a mortar and pestle (or a bowl to crush seeds).

Method:

Using the mortar and pestle, crush the seeds into powder, enjoying the whiff of fresh herbs as you do this. Add the ginger, salt, turmeric and mix all the ingredients together. Be careful adding the chili; not everybody loves spicy, but add a teaspoon to the mixture for moderate heat. If you love hot spicy paste, add as much as you like, and I suggest some cool yogurt dressing to accompany the dish.

Use it immediately, although you can store the mixture for up to four weeks.

DILL

is traditionally used in gripe water, a medicine that has relieved teething problems in young children for hundreds of years. Its effect is to soothe the gums and aid sleep. Dill has a gentle flavor and delicate, feathery leaves. However, I advise that dill be used on its own, as more potent herbs will overwhelm its flavor.

Dill is often used with eggs, and I love dill on pancakes with honey. Fresh or dried, it adds a unique taste sensation, and I don't add sugar because the honey provides enough sweetness. These no-sugar dill and honey pancakes are an example of the versatility of dill when combined with sweet flavors.

You will need:

- one cup of plain flour
- one cup of milk
- 30 grams of butter
- one egg
- some oil to fry the pancakes
- honey, and
- a teaspoon of dill leaves

Method:

Soften the butter for 15-20 minutes before use. While you're waiting, break the egg into a cup, whisk it, and add to a bowl. Mix the softened butter with the egg, and then add the milk and flour. Cream in the dill leaves; they add a feathery texture to the mix, and they infuse your pancake with its scent. Put some oil in a frying pan and allow it to heat up for a minute, then pour a cup of the mixture into the pan and let it cook gently until the edges turn a slightly golden brown. Flip the pancake! This is always fun with young children. At this stage, I like to add the honey into the center so that it heats up, but you can add this later if you prefer. If you want soggy pancakes, remove them quicker than if you like crispy ones; for these, keep cooking until the edges turn brown. Finally, roll the pancake and put it on a plate. If you are the cook, you will find it difficult to resist, so make sure you do a taste test. That dill will not shout at you, but it certainly is noticeable. Enjoy.

Fennel

has a robust aniseed flavor evident in the leaves and the seeds. Fennel is an ingredient in Absinthe, the famous drink of the Belle Époque in France, consumed by artists such as Picasso, Van Gogh, and Toulouse-Lautrec. In those days, it was the recommended drink for treating epilepsy. However, nowadays it is not recommended for this use!

Fennel survives the winter outside, and its seeds are used to flavor bread and add a licorice flavor for culinary use in savory egg and cheese tarts. If you have fennel in your garden, you can enjoy fresh leaves all winter long. This herb provides fresh greens when few are available, and the seed heads can be collected as you need them.

Garlic

is famous for having medicinal benefits, and many doctors recommend taking garlic capsules. I have friends who eat a clove of fresh garlic daily, but the smell on your breath can be a bit off-putting for work colleagues, so maybe do this on weekends. Traditionally garlic is reputed to reduce cholesterol and blood pressure. You can make garlic-infused oil, and it is wonderful but be careful with how long you keep it as it tends to go rancid quickly once opened. Instead, store it in the refrigerator and discard it after about 4-5 days, especially if it smells bad.

Garlic soup is a French recipe that tourists can enjoy on holiday or which you can recreate in your kitchen. The strong taste is reduced by cooking, and the flavor is unbeatable on a cold winter's evening.

You will need:

- 5 bulbs of garlic (which you will separate into individual cloves)
- a liter of water (or slightly more if you have a lot of guests)
- 2-3 slices of bread made into bread crumbs
- a sprig of thyme, and
- some grated cheese and black pepper as a topping

Method:

Add the cloves and a bay leaf to a liter of water – no need to take off the skins; they will slip off after 30 mins in boiling water. Then remove the pot from the boil, take off the skins and discard them. Mash the garlic at this stage, or use a food processor if you like. Next, add herbs like thyme and other Mediterranean herbs. Tarragon is terrific in this if you have some fresh leaves to pick. Finally, add salt and pepper and bread crumbs and allow the soup

The Essesntial Herb Gardening Handbook

to simmer on warm heat. (You can pour your friends a herb cocktail in this interval). Before serving, remove the bay leaf, add parsley and grated cheddar as a topping, and there you go. Garlic soup! I like to serve it with homemade garlic bread if you have the time and patience.

Lavender

is used all over the work as an aid for relaxing. Added to soaps, bath oils, and many herbal bubble baths, this herb is famous for helping you sleep. A sprig of lavender in a clothing drawer allows the scent to permeate the fabric over time. It is a beautiful addition to a funeral bouquet, as the smell spreads through the ceremony, soothing all present. Here is an easy way to make lavender oil.

You will need:

A recycled clean glass container, 12 sprigs of freshly cut lavender, some base oil – olive is fine for this, but you can shop in your local health food store. Almond oil is also extraordinarily sweet-smelling, and the lavender will add an extra scent.

Method:

Sterilize the glass container by washing in the dishwasher or placing it in a bowl of hot water and drying it off in the oven for a few minutes. Then half fill the jar with your chosen oil. Cut the flowers from the stems and add them to the oil, then top up the jar with oil to the top. Allow to sit in a shady place for 4-5 days, then remove the flowers and add new ones. You will need to change the flowers at least three times for the scent to remain. Then close up your jar and store it in a dark cupboard or your bathroom. Add 8-12 drops at bath time for a relaxing soak after a hard day's work or energetic sports.

Lemon Balm

Tea made from its leaves is said to settle a sick stomach, especially nerves before an exam, a driving test, or whatever makes you nervous! Collect fresh leaves if available; if not, use dried leaves you saved during the summer. Lemon Balm tea used to be a remedy for feverish colds in the UK, and its lemon scent adds a delicious reminder of summer in a basket full of dried herbs in a bathroom or hallway.

For many ideas here, you need to dry some herb leaves. To do this, dry leaves, pick several stems with a lot of foliage and use the stem to hang them to dry in a shady area until you need them.

You can tie the stems with string and then hang them upside down to dry. Above a fridge is a good location, as the area is usually cozy. The herb leaves begin to turn a brown color which tells you the goodness within them is being retained. When you need some leaves, just pick them from a stem. The scent will fill the whole area but be careful not to place bay and lavender too close to more delicate tastes. These powerful scents will dominate some subtler flavors like French Tarragon.

Marjoram

is famed for its fantastic taste in French and Italian cooking, this herb has also been used for years to soothe aching joints and conditions related to inflammation. Like lavender, marjoram oil can be soothing on painful joints. Make oil in the same way as lavender oil, and then use a few drops in bathwater or on a compress to help soothe aching joints and muscles after a long day in your garden. Marjoram and oregano can be used interchangeably in recipes – if no fresh leaves are available, make sure you dry some in summer so that you can add them to winter dishes.

Mint

can be used in tea to ease morning sickness in some women and is even better if combined with ginger. In fact, for nausea of any type, if you smell a drop of mint or ginger oil onto a tissue, it usually helps. In addition, mint is a traditional aid to ease flatulence in some cultures. Perhaps this is why the fresh leaves are often offered after a meal has finished, accompanied by fennel seeds, and with chocolates, mint provides after-dinner relief. Of course, another reason may be the fresh taste its leaves bring in the mouth, as most of us are used to the taste of mint in toothpaste.

Peppermint tea is recognized as a drink to cool people down in hot weather, and many discover drinking too much causes them to feel cold, so don't drink too many cups even if it is very hot! Mint tea can be made in advance and left in a jug in the fridge for when you need a cooling drink on a hot day. Finally, mint is a common herb that you find in every cocktail bar, and its green leaves often adorn the edge of a glass. Crème de menthe is a popular alcoholic French drink that is now drunk worldwide.

To make peppermint tea at home, make sure you dry some of the leaves before the plant dies off for the winter. See how to do this in Lemon Balm above. You can pick as many as possible, then hang them to dry in a shady corner. Then add a few fresh or dried leaves to some boiling water whenever you need a refreshing drink and sit down for a few moments of peace.

Oregano

like marjoram, is useful for adding flavor to soups and winter stews. You can dry the leaves when it is growing well in summer for use in winter. Oregano is excellent added to stuffing mixtures for festive occasions and is often combined with thyme or sage.

Parsley

can be used like celery seed, and the fresh leaves of parsley tea reputedly help remove toxins from the system. Chop a teaspoon of fresh parsley and cover with boiling water to make a pleasant tea. However, dried parsley never gives me the same satisfaction as the fresh herb, so I recommend a late sowing of parsley in August so that you can pick the fresh herb indoors for winter use.

The Essesntial Herb Gardening Handbook

Rosemary

for remembrance, the old saying goes. Although delicious in taste, rosemary oil is not recommended for anybody in the first months of pregnancy or for people with high blood pressure. This is because some herb oils affect the uterine muscles, and rosemary is one of these. However, its scent offers users an uplifting aroma, as any gardener knows as they pass by the herb in the outdoors.

The smell can outdo other herbs in cooking, so use it sparingly. However, it is delicious if added to a sprig of herbs such as thyme and sage and used to make vegetable stock for soups and stews.

Rosemary alcohol tincture is often recommended as an aid to improve circulation. Chat to your doctor first and if they agree, rub it into affected areas such as legs that are tired or have varicose veins. Traditionally, rosemary is an antiseptic oil, and its strong flavor can be recognized in the world-famous Benedectine liqueur.

Sage

is a strong-smelling herb, best grown apart from many plants, although it grows well with strawberries and even borage. The medical profession has been testing the quality of sage oil for many digestive conditions, and the common belief is that sage oil helps reduce excessive perspiration. The leaves are high in vitamins A and C and also contain a high amount of vitamin K.

Its extremely strong flavor is used in conjunction with other Mediterranean herbs like oregano, garlic, dill, parsley, marjoram, and thyme to make a herb-based stock. Stock adds body to many cooked soups and stews, and you can make it when the herbs are ready, then freeze it for use later on in the year. If you have old yogurt or cream pots, these are fabulous to store stock. Make sure you label it!

You will need:

A handful of herb leaves, including 3-4 sage leaves, a sprig of thyme, a bay leaf, a sprig of rosemary, and then any others you have available – marjoram, parsley, etc. An onion, chopped, three cloves of garlic, some water to boil the herbs, and salt and pepper to taste.

Method:

Chop the garlic and onion and fry this in a bit of vegetable oil to start. Fine chop all the herbs as this will release the flavor. Add these to the garlic and onion mixture and add a liter of water (top up as required). For non-vegetarians, if you have any leftover chicken bones, these can be added to make a rich taste to this stock but make sure you do not add this to dishes if you have vegetarian or vegan guests. Allow the mixture to bubble away. If you use bones, allow to cook for at least 30 mins, but for herb stock, about 20-30 minutes if perfect. Then let the mixture cool, pour into pots, and freeze until you need it. Add this to any stew or soup where the flavor of herbs adds depth to your cooking.

Winter Savory

offers leaves to the cook when there are very few growing, so this one is so worth including in the garden. Also, perhaps because it was so important historically, the leaves and stems were used to make teas and tonics, which were believed to help indigestion and nausea. Nowadays, some herbalists recommend its use as a natural remedy for winter coughs and colds that are hard to shift but take the advice of a professional or your chemist on this.

Summer Savory

adds a unique flavor to summer salads. Still, it also has a history of usage as an anti-inflammatory and antimicrobial herb derived from oil-soaked in the leaves. You can make your own oil in the same way suggested for lavender above and try this in the same way – to apply to sore muscles. Some herbalists recommend this for internal use, so please discuss this with your doctor. The Romans reputedly believed that this herb was an aphrodisiac. However, I can only sing the praises for the fantastic, fresh taste the leaves offer to many dishes and leave you to decide if the claims have any truth in them!

Tarragon

is an ingredient in many French dishes, but here I must recommend the qualities of the fresh herb. One hint from midwives was that eating tarragon used to bring on menstruation, and it is also said to aid digestion.

This is one of my absolute favorites and is not very well-known due to its inability to grow from seed. However, it is so worth getting a plant, and from here on in, you can propagate it, look after it, and spread this herb joy among friends and family.

No other herb tastes like tarragon. Just a tiny amount of it in soups, egg dishes, and cooked tarts make it an essential herb in my garden.

In France, it makes Bearnaise sauce and tarragon vinegar. For me, this is the perfect topping for scrambled eggs, as it releases its fresh, slightly licorice flavor through every mouthful. Here is how to make the perfect tarragon scrambled eggs.

You will need:

- a small teaspoon of butter
- 2 eggs beaten in a cup of milk
- some fresh tarragon leaves (dried leaves will have to do if no fresh ones are available), and
- black pepper to taste

Method:

Heat and melt a tiny amount of butter in a pan, and then add the eggs and milk mixture, stirring continuously. Chop the tarragon into small pieces and add this to the mixture.

The eggs will thicken naturally; add more milk if it is too thick. Serve immediately on hot toast with black pepper.

THYME

thrives in low fertility soil, almost a herb of neglect. You can pick thyme all winter long, so there is no need to dry leaves. The cheerful pink flowers are a magnet for bees, and I use this herb in dishes that need slow cooking because its taste infuses the dish that way.

There are many studies involving the compounds contained in thyme-infused oil. Thymol, linalool, and camphor are some of the elements. In European monasteries, it was believed that thyme was an anti-bacterial oil that could effectively preserve food, and treat stomach pains from eating spoiled food. Nowadays, there are also studies investigating thyme oil to promote healthy hair growth.

Whatever the case for the medical benefits of this gorgeous herb, I think it adds a unique, exceptional taste to squash soup.

You will need:

- 1 squash, cut into pieces with skin intact and seeds removed
- 2 cloves of garlic, chopped
- an onion
- some vegetable stock
- several sprigs of thyme and a bay leaf
- salt and pepper to taste, and
- natural yogurt to serve on top with a garnish of either parsley or whatever fresh herb is available.

Method:

Partially cook the squash in the oven for about 25 minutes until it is soft. While it is cooking, start frying the garlic and onion in a pan. Remove the cooked squash from the oven and add them to the pan with a liter of water, a bay leaf, and the sprigs of thyme. A pinch of salt and pepper added here will add to the flavor. Then allow the soup to cook slowly on low heat. When the squash is cooked through (after 20-30 minutes), add the vegetable stock and simmer on low heat for another 5 minutes. Then serve in bowls, with natural yogurt and cheese with a fresh herb topping like parsley.

The Essesntial Herb Gardening Handbook

ON A FINAL NOTE, THERE ARE MANY EXAMPLES OF HERBS USED IN alcoholic drinks, such as the famous Chartreuse green liqueur and, more recently, herbs infused in gin, adding a rich dimension to the taste. In medicine, many studies are trying to prove the abilities that humanity has attributed to various herbs. Hopefully, this chapter has inspired you to learn more about what herbs contain and how they can be used in your daily life. In the next chapter, we will examine what could go wrong when growing herbs and how to fix these problems.

Chapter 7
What Could Go Wrong? (and how to fix it)

In this chapter, we examine some of the typical problems that occur with herb plants and suggest ways to fix them.

1. **Roots:** root rot, eelworm, vine weevil.
2. **Leaves:** yellowing leaves, brown spots, leaf curl, wilting leaves, leaf rust, and leaf mold (botrytis).
3. **Stem:** Brown stem, stem rot, damping-off fungi, scale insects, mealybugs.
4. **Growth:** slow growth, excessive leaf foliage.
5. **Flowers:** lack of flowers, feeding flowers, flowers go to seed.
6. **Pests:** aphids, caterpillars, earwigs, greenfly, slugs, snails, whitefly, red spider mite, scale insects.

Some problems with herbs may be due to a lack of nutrients in the soil. Composting, mulching, leaf mold, and crop rotation can help with any nutrient-related issues; see more below.

∽

1. Problems with roots

Root rot refers to healthy roots becoming pot-bound or water-logged, leading to brown, diseased roots. Healthy roots should be white or cream colored. *Oregano* and *thyme* are both prone to root rot if conditions are damp and drainage is poor.

If roots start to lose their natural shape growing straight downwards, as they would in the ground, it is called being **pot-bound**. Often pot-bound roots make a plant unstable, and it keeps falling over. Being pot-bound means the roots start to curl around the end of the pot. This does not make for good drainage, so it is best to re-pot this herb.

To examine the roots of the herb in a pot, soak the pot in a bucket of water for at least 15 minutes to loosen up the roots and then turn the pot upside down. Place your hand around the stem so that it falls gently into your palm, and then lay the plant out on a cloth or recycled paper to take a look. Root rot is often preceded by the roots becoming bound by the edges of a pot that is too small. Support the plant in your hand while you tease out the roots and try to aim them vertically downwards. This will help the roots grow naturally as soon as they are planted.

Now is the time to remove any brown or black roots using cleaned cutting shears or a pruner. Clean the blade before each cut to avoid spreading diseases.

How do I know if my herb is pot-bound?

- You can see tiny roots at the end of the pot when you look at it.
- The whole plant guzzles water – and dries out again really quickly.
- The whole plant looks unhealthy, there is not a lot of

new growth at the tips, and overall, leaf growth is extremely slow.

How do I fix it?

Pot-bound roots are curled in the shape of the pot, so you need to tease these out carefully. Soaking the plant in water for an hour will aid this process. Try to ease roots into a vertical direction, and shape them into how you imagine the roots of a tree grow underground – expanding sideways and downwards. If you find any brown or black roots, your herb has root rot.

How do I fix root rot?

To treat root rot, use a sterile cutting knife or pruning shears and cut all the diseased roots off. Wipe down the blade before each cut so that you do not spread disease. If the remaining roots look a healthy white or cream color, allow them to dry for a few hours and then re-pot them into a bigger pot with fresh compost. Do not overwater this plant again, and keep an eye for new leaves to ensure it makes a full recovery.

If your herb is in soil, dig around the roots gently with a stick or trowel and examine the roots. If you see black or brown, you need to dig out the herb immediately. Feel the soil around the roots. Is it very moist? You know what the problem is here! Over-watering. Remember, many herbs survive well on rainfall alone, so stop watering for several days, and then check the soil for dryness before you water again.

Root rot is a serious condition, and your herb plant will not survive if you continue as usual. Check again how often your herb needs to be watered, and then favor not watering if you are in doubt. French Tarragon is prone to root rot in very heavy soils, so make sure the soil you provide has some sand, gravel, and humus to avoid it.

Other problems with roots are usually caused by eelworm or vine weevils. See pests below for how to treat these.

2. PROBLEMS WITH LEAVES

- **Yellowing leaves** are often a sign that your herb has been getting too much water. Has somebody been looking after your herb while you went on holiday? Excessive overwatering can result in yellow leaves. Another culprit could be aphids eating the leaves. See more on pests below. If the herb is also showing roots at the end of the pot, it usually means the whole herb needs to be repotted and given more nutrition via the soil. Yellow leaves on herbs planted in the ground can also indicate that the herb is coming to the end of its natural life if it is an annual plant. Basil leaves often start to look paler from late August onwards.

How do I fix it?

Hard water can be the culprit too, so if your tap water is hard, run it through a filter or use saved rainwater.

Yellow coloring between the veins can indicate a shortage of trace elements like nitrogen in your soil. See more on this in Number 7 below.

Brown spots on leaves are often the result of under-watering, and pests cause leaves to look mottled and unhealthy. Another possible is too much sun, but this is unlikely for most herbs that crave a lot of sunshine. *Mint* and *Lemon balm* leaves may turn brown in too much sunshine, but the problem is likely one of the above.

The Essesntial Herb Gardening Handbook

If under-watering is the problem, water the plant well and see if it recovers. If so, continue to water more regularly and pick leaves too. Pick the brown leaves off, and regular picking will encourage healthy growth. Pests may be aphids and greenflies – see how to deal with these below.

Consult the guide to the best conditions again. For example, if the herb likes shade, make sure it is in the shade at the hottest part of the day.

- **Leaf curl** tends to happen when there is a sudden drop in temperature or a lack of manganese in the soil.

How do I fix it?

If your plant is indoors, is it in a draft? Has the weather changed recently? If the herb is outdoors, check the location. For example, maybe you moved the herb to a larger pot, which exposed the herb to drafts or blocked the sunlight it was used to. Move the herb to a more sheltered location out of drafts and then leave it for a few weeks to recover. If the fall is approaching, maybe it is time for the plant to move indoors.

If it lacks manganese, then try feeding using a fertilizer mix in your watering can. If it helps and the plant improves, feed the herb monthly.

- **Wilting leaves** can show that your plant is not being watered enough; this is easy to spot with parsley, basil, and cilantro when the whole plant seems to collapse.

How do I fix it?

First, water the plants generously and see if it recovers. After this, water more regularly!

- **Leaf rust** is exceptionally unusual on herbs. It presents as small round patches of brown rings on the underside of the herb's leaves. It usually indicates not enough sunshine combined with excessive watering.

How do I fix it?

If you can, move the herb to a sunnier spot, remove the affected leaves and limit your zeal for watering this herb.

- **Leaf mold**, or **botyritis**, commonly affects cucumber plants, so if your herbs are in close proximity, there may be a danger of them coming into contact with affected leaves. This is a gray, soft, fluffy mold that attacks large cucumber leaves but spreads easily to other parts and plants nearby. Basil is very susceptible to this.

How do I fix it?

The affected leaves should be removed immediately with gloves and destroyed. Do not add these to compost bins! Try to improve the airflow to get rid of leaf mold; it spreads in damp conditions too, so avoid overwatering plants for a spell.

- **Holes in leaves** can be a result of flea beetles, earwigs, and caterpillars, so see the section on pests below.

3. Stem problems

- A **brown color** that appears on a normally green stem is sometimes caused by overwatering the plant and leaving moisture on its leaves. It sometimes occurs in the middle of the stem, and the gardener feels as if the plant is dying. The cause may be too much watering and where you water.

How do I fix it?

Try to aim for the soil around the stem when you water and not the leaves or the actual stem. Leaving drops of water on the leaves or stems higher up is not ideal for most herbs, which usually prefer some sunshine and drier conditions.

- Sometimes a **brown stem** can indicate a lack of calcium, often spotted on the tomato plants growing beside basil, cilantro, parsley, and chives.

How do I fix it?

In this case, you can save eggshells and crush them once they have dried. Place them at the base of the stem of the affected plants. The eggshells will slowly release calcium (via the keratin in eggshells), which will help the tomatoes recover gradually. Some gardeners also use crushed eggshells, with spiky edges to persuade slugs and snail visitors not to nibble the surrounding plants.

- **Damage from pests** is another possibility. Pests like leather jackets like stems and roots. They are gray creatures, about an inch long, and they thrive in light soils and very moist soil.

How do I fix it?

Keep the soil dry for a while and remove them if you see them. They are an unusual and challenging pest because you rarely see them, as they live underground.

4. PROBLEMS WITH GROWTH

- Why is my **herb growing so slowly**?

First, check the predicted height of your herb. Some herbs do not grow very tall, and summer savory and tarragon are often weeded out by inexperienced gardeners because they "look like a weed". The following reason may be insufficient sunshine or a lack of trace elements in the soil. It may be that another plant is shading your herb for a lot of the active, sunny hours in the day? Next, check the season. If it is September or October, it is possible that the herb has reached the end of its life cycle or that it is going into a dormant phase for the winter. If it is still mid-summer, there may be a pest lurking.

How do I fix it?

Usually, I recommend turning the pot upside down, holding it carefully in your hand, and checking the roots. If the roots are pot-bound, you need to tease the roots out gently by soaking them in water. Then, replace the pot with a bigger one and give it fresh soil. This should provide your herb with excellent conditions to start growing bigger.

Try moving the herb into more direct sunshine (not shade-loving herbs, though, like mint or Lemon balm). If the plant recovers, leave it in the new location. See more about soil and nutrients in Number 7 below.

A final solution could be a massive aphid infestation. First, check for a sticky residue on the leaves or brown patches on the undersides. If this is the case, then wipe the leaves with some dish soap in water applied with a soft cloth.

- What herbs **survive the winter**?

To survive, some herbs need to be taken indoors as soon as the temperature plunges. Tarragon and lovage are two of these.

Some herbs are annuals and only last one growing season, such as basil, coriander, and parsley.

Frost hardy herbs.

However, some herbs are fine outdoors even in winter, and you can continue picking leaves throughout the winter season. These include Bay leaf, sage, mint, rosemary, and thyme, which will all be fine outdoors.

5. Problems with flowers

Flowers are a part of the herb's life cycle. Starting with a seed that germinates in soil, the plant produces green foliage with aromatic tastes and smells, and then it flowers to be pollinated, and then it goes to seed. Some herbs have flowers that pollinators adore, such as sage, rosemary, thyme, and lavender. Bees will flock to your garden, as will butterflies, to enjoy their nectar. Flowers are a sign that the herb has finished its growing cycle and has decided to finish its life cycle.

- **Going to seed**: Basil and cilantro are notorious for this! Both have attractive flowers, but to extend the plant's life cycle for foliage, remove the flowers and add them to salads or as a garnish on soups. Chives usually go to seed at the end of a season. They offer a dash of circular purple flowers to any flower bed they are in, and usually, they will return the following year. Just enjoy the color!

How do I fix it?

Often, the reason is the herb's natural life-cycle but is increased by a lack of water or a lack of nutrients in the soil. If you want to keep picking leaves from your herbs, then cut the flowers and re-pot the herb. Give it a thorough watering, and this gives the herb a new lease of life.

To prevent this, cut the seed heads as they develop or cut the flowers for display inside because the scent of the foliage will add a delicious fragrance to your flower arrangements.

If you want to collect the seed, coriander is collected from cilantro herbs for culinary use, so do not remove the flowers and allow the herb to seed. Collect them in a paper envelope to dry them out well, then store them in the kitchen in a spice jar.

French tarragon rarely flowers, so do not be disappointed. Its Russian cousin does flower profusely, and if you let it go to seed, it will happily spread through a shady area of your garden and even become invasive.

- If **no flowers** develop at all, you may have an aphid problem. These devour the tips of herbs, including aromatic flower buds and flowers.

How do I fix this?

Dish soap and water is an easy method - see how to remove them below. Some gardeners use neem oil and water, and others recommend citrus oil.

6. WHAT PESTS TARGET HERBS?

- **Aphids** love a variety of plants and can be spotted by the sticky residue they deposit on plant leaves. Herbs they target include almost all of them apart from herbs with a strong scent like chives, garlic, tarragon, and lavender. Also known as greenflies, these pests attack growing tips, and flowers are their favorite. Every experienced gardener has a tale about greenfly, or blackfly, or even orange fly raiding the leaves and flowers of their favorite rose, geranium, and any flowering tip they find.

How do I fix it?

The pest depletes the strength of the whole plant, so physically remove them using a tablespoon of dish soap added to a watering can full of water, then apply to the affected area with a soft sponge or cloth.

- **Scale insects** love the long, thin leaves of tarragon, but they also enjoy Bay leaf and many other indoor house plants, so check the undersides of leaves for brown shades that are difficult to remove. Be careful when bringing herbs back in for winter. Check for scale insects before they come in, or they will spread like wildfire among your favorite house plants.

How do I fix it?

These insects stick to the back of the leaves, and they have to be removed one by one in a long, painful process. If you miss even one, you will be back to this again in 6 months! On tarragon, they are not difficult to locate. Often I just cut the leaf off and dispose of the whole leaf and any insects.

- **Red spider mite** prefers dry, warm conditions, and herbs in a greenhouse often fit this bill, so remove the bugs with a mixture of 1 tablespoon of dish soap in a liter of water. Add this to a spray bottle and aim it directly at the red spots on the leaves.

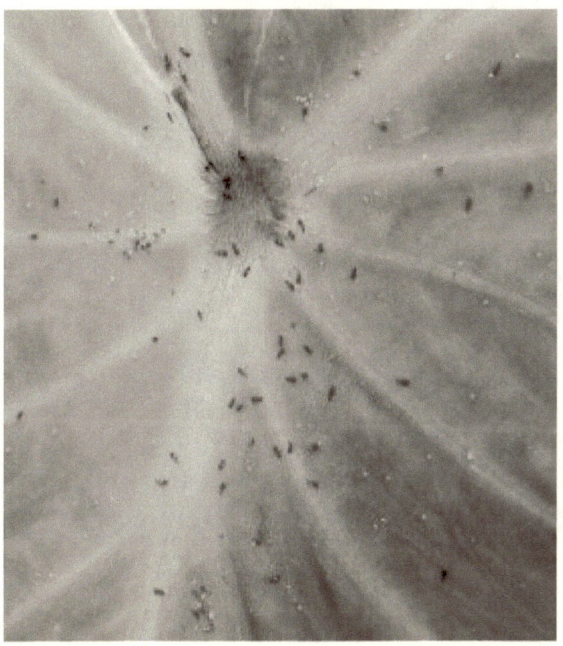

How do I fix it?

Spray the pests, then wipe the leaves down with a damp sponge or cloth. This bug hates to be damp, so it should leave. To keep it away long-term, water the herb more frequently for a while and spray the leaves if affected. Then wipe them down with a cloth. Aerate the whole area, too, because red spider mites like dry, warm conditions, and if you keep it damp and drafty, they can be encouraged to abandon the plant.

- **Leafhoppers** and **leaf-miners**. If you see trails, or tunnels, on basil leaves, you may have leafhoppers nearby. These pests also enjoy munching oregano and parsley, and these herbs often grow close to each other.

How do I fix it?

Plant lots of extra herbs. These bugs are challenging to eliminate, but if you have extra herbs, they can munch on some, and you still have lots of foliage to pick.

- **Slugs** and **snails** eat any tiny seedlings, and they prefer fresh green leaves from new growth.

How do I fix it?

These two pests are the scourge of gardeners, and there are millions of ideas from beer traps to eggshells, but some possible ideas include

1. Cut bramble pieces and surround your herb plants with these. Physical spikes often send these slimy pests searching for more accessible food supplies. The sharp edges of eggshell pieces can also deter them.
2. Use leaves as decoy bait! Comfrey or nasturtium leaves are a favorite of these slugs, but if they are super hungry, you may still find them on the herbs in the morning.
3. Physically remove them. Get handy with a flashlight late at night and go slime detective hunting. If you find

some, relocate them to your compost bin where they can decompose plants that need it.

A final note: If you develop a fool-proof method to keep slugs and snails away, you are destined to become a millionaire and to be loved by every gardener in the world.

The Essesntial Herb Gardening Handbook

- **Eelworm** and **vine weevils** attack the roots of plants. In addition, many herb leaves exude an aromatic fragrance that keeps airborne pests at bay, but the roots of any plant are vulnerable to these two.

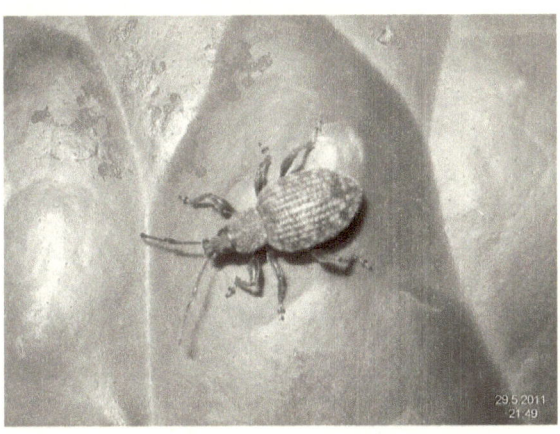

How do I fix it?

This is extremely difficult as you need to access the roots. If the herb is in a pot, upend it carefully to sneak a look at the roots. Are there bulbous swellings in the roots? This is definitely eelworm. There is no saving this herb, and the important thing is to dispose of the plant safely.

Vine weevils devour the whole root system, causing the herb to collapse, which is also impossible to save. The best idea is to buy sterilized compost in the future. A cold spell will kill these pests, but if your herbs are in the soil, it may be worth transferring them to pots for one season, using fresh compost, and then covering the infected area.

If you also grow vines, plant your herbs some distance away from them to avoid this problem.

- **Caterpillars**, **earwigs**, and **flea beetles** eat small or large holes in leaves. Butterfly lovers may be delighted to see wildlife in their garden.

How do I fix it?

You can don some gloves and move caterpillars to other plants if you prefer to allow them to continue their life cycle. I recommend this, by the way. Most butterfly and moth species are in trouble, and allowing a few of them to munch on your plants will also bring some spectacular pollinators to admire on your flowers later on.

Earwigs are challenging to catch, but if you and a partner work together, they can be teased into collecting jars and placed back in compost bins.

Flea beetles do not like soap and water mixtures sprayed on the leaves, and they can also be lured onto sticky traps. So if you use this method, remember to wash edible herbs before use.

7. LACK OF NUTRIENTS. IMPROVE THE SOIL FOR YOUR HERBS.

In Chapter 5 we looked at different ways to improve the soil, so please refer back to that for information about composting, mulching, and using leaf mold. Companion planting for herbs discussed in Chapter 4 will be helpful to decide which herbs to plant together. Finally, this section will examine the benefits of crop rotation in a growing plan for a garden over a four-year period and how this can boost your soil and ultimately help your herbs thrive.

First, let's see which nutrients are needed in the soil where your herbs will grow. If you have ever bought a bag of plant fertilizer, you will see these letters in brackets in the ingredients on the packaging, sometimes labeled as NPK feeds. See what these letters mean below!

- Nitrogen (N) is the leaf maker of your herb. It is used for plants to photosynthesize, that is, to make food from sunshine using their leaves. If there isn't enough nitrogen available, the leaves may be yellow and the overall growth of your herb may be less than you would like.
- Phosphorus (P) is what gives the roots their healthy glow.
- Potassium (K) is needed for flowers and helps the herb utilize nitrogen. This is the element that keeps the stem healthy, which then strengthens the whole plant. Leaves are often mottled with strange patterns if potassium is missing from the soil.
- Calcium (Ca). Without this nutrient in the soil, the whole plant can die because it adjusts the acidity, enabling nutrient absorption.
- Magnesium (Mg) is one nutrient that helps the initial

germination of the seed and helps the herb produce chlorophyll. Without this, leaves can fall off the plant.

There are other parts of fertile soil called trace elements or minerals. These are often called minor elements because the main growth elements are the ones above. However, without these in the soil, your herbs will not thrive.

- Iron (Fe) is used to make chlorophyll, the food a plant uses to grow. Without it, leaves are pale or yellow. Think of a human who needs an iron tonic, and you get the idea!
- Manganese (Mn) is essential to avoid curling leaves, which are often pale in color. Fe and Mn are used to form chlorophyll.
- Boron (B) (or the lack of it) is the culprit when you notice brown centers in a vegetable and also causes patches on leaves and fruit. If there is a supply of boron in the soil, other nutrients are absorbed efficiently.
- Molybdenum (Mo) is present in the soil that has added lime, and it ensures that nitrogen is available for the herb to use. The growing tips will look malformed without this trace element, so it is an essential part of your soil.
- Copper (Cu) is essential, especially for the young plant, and it gives a boost to the whole herb when it is present. Leaves may wilt without it.
- Zinc (Zn) is a big helper in plant nutrition. Chlorophyll, several proteins, and carbohydrates are not formed well without zinc. Many commercial fertilizers contain high levels of phosphorous, which then makes it more difficult for the herb to use zinc. So try to add compost to the soil, which aids zinc availability.

The Essesntial Herb Gardening Handbook

What is crop rotation?

Crop rotation is a method devised by farmers who noticed that growing the same plant in the same ground year after year resulted in poorer yields, depletion of the soil, and often allowed diseases and pests to take hold in the soil. The basic idea is that some plants take a lot of energy from the soil and deplete certain nutrients. Instead of continuing to add manure or compost to replace those, the next set of plants can add those things to the soil instead. For example, beans and peas can add nitrogen back into the soil, which the cabbage family loves. So if you plant cabbages after a season of peas, the cabbage will benefit from the peas planted before it.

Even if you plan to grow herbs in pots, use this same idea for not growing the same herb in the same pot if it is an annual. Change the crop so that the soil gets a different herb, and you can keep topping up the fertility of your pots by adding mulches, compost, leaf mold, and wood ash.

This is a 4-year plan. For example, if you plant potatoes in year 1, they will not be planted again in the same ground until year 5. The herbs you choose can work with many of the crops listed below, but this is a guide to vegetable and fruit growing which will help you decide which herbs can be planted alongside your vegetables. Please refer back to companion planting for each individual herb in Chapter 4.

Crop Rotation and where to fit your herbs

Year 1

Fertilizer

Manure in spring. Compost mixed into manure will improve soil texture too. Plant feeds are required in summer.

Plants

Potatoes and 'hungry' plants like eggplant, radishes, tomatoes, squashes, pumpkins, zucchini, and cucumber

Herbs

Basil, parsley, chives, cilantro, and oregano. Bay leaf is an option, but it may be too big to be a permanent companion.

Notes

Potatoes "clear" the ground. The others are very hungry, annual plants. Feed them weekly when flowering and fruiting in summer.

Watering

All the vegetable plants need a lot of regular watering. Include special feeds such as nettle, comfrey, dandelion leaves to help them grow better. Use herbs that enjoy these conditions.

Year 2

Fertilizer

Manure in spring. Add general compost too. Fertilize with plant feeds every 2-3 weeks.

Plants

Legumes, or a mix of peas, beans, and onions.

Herbs

Garlic, chives, and summer savory. If you plant broad beans, consider adding fennel to attract blackflies.

Notes

Nitrogen fixers that will feed the Brassicas which follow. These can all be planted separately.

The Essesntial Herb Gardening Handbook

Watering

All need regular watering. Can be enriched with comfrey or nettle leaves and feed.

Year 3

Fertilizer

Lime is needed (or slightly acid soil) for Brassicas to grow well. Do not manure. Apply general compost—mulch with leaf mold.

Plants

Brassicas – Cabbage family (Brussels sprouts, cauliflower, broccoli, cabbage)

Herbs

Nasturtiums. Aphids will go directly to the leaves and flowers, not your vegetables: chives, savory, cilantro, and oregano. Marigolds and mint reputedly deter cabbage root fly.

Notes

Do not manure - plant with leaf mold and comfrey leaves in the bed, which decompose during the season. They love nitrogen from peas and beans.

Watering

Make sure the soil is firm around young plants. Then, they can be moved from a nursery bed to a permanent bed in autumn.

Year 4

Fertilizer

Do not manure. Spread general compost. Remove stones.

Plants

Roots (carrots, bets, turnips, parsnips).

Herbs

Chives (to distract pests), parsley, marjoram.

Notes

Do not manure - it will cause the roots to split. Remove large stones, or roots will grow around them!

Watering

Water well to improve germination. May need protective netting.

Perennial Crops

Fertilizer

All benefit from manure. Fruit and asparagus love ash (from fires) as fertilizer – spread in winter to boost growth

Plants

Strawberries, raspberries, fruit bushes, asparagus.

Herbs

Sage, basil, mint, lemon balm.

Notes

Move the fruit every 3-4 years or when fruiting stops. Asparagus can stay in the same place for up to 25 years.

Watering

Water these plants only in spring and summer.

General guidelines for healthy herbs.

- Try to give herbs the optimum conditions – direct sunlight or semi-shade as appropriate, suitable soil and not crowd them altogether. Allow some air to circulate between them for best results.
- Try to pick them regularly. Otherwise, several herbs tend to "bolt", which means if it is basil or cilantro, they flower then go to seed about a month after germination. If you pick them often, you will notice any pests, brown leaves, or drooping branches, and you can take action. Prune any branches that look too heavy or spoil the overall shape.
- Weed between them and remove dead leaves to help stop the pests from arriving. Slugs and snails often move in to munch on decaying leaves, and other pests will do the same. Weed out any unintended plants and pick your herbs.
- Know how much water they need, and then make sure the ones that need water get watered regularly. This stops them from going to seed early. Feel the soil before you water. Without disturbing the roots, dig with your finger and see if the soil an inch down seems dry too. If so, water! Herbs like this include basil, chives, cilantro, and garlic.
- If you know a herb does not need much water, then place it further away from the tap, and you are less likely to have a full watering can when you get there. Herbs like this include mint, lemon balm, lavender, sage, rosemary, and thyme. These usually survive on sparse rainfall in Mediterranean climates and go for a long time without water. So you really only need to water these if they are visibly wilting in a heatwave.

- Include sweet scents like lavender, lemon balm, rosemary, and thyme. You will enjoy walking past these herbs, and the bees and butterflies will visit your garden a lot more.
- Finally, decoy flowers and leaves like nasturtiums and comfrey are a natural way to keep pests off your precious plants. Both of these have flowers that bees love too, so they are a colorful addition to a herb garden.

Chapter 8
Cooking with Herbs

WHILE COOKING IS MORE ART THAN SCIENCE, YOU CAN STILL follow some basic rules and techniques. Start with the basics here, and as you learn how these flavors work and interact with each other, you can branch out and get more creative.

First, identify the type of cuisine you are cooking. If you aren't sure what region or style your recipe is from, don't worry; just compare the flavors in the recipe for the main dish against the flavor summary table further on in this chapter. If you still aren't sure what to do, check the individual herb cheat sheets and pick something with a flavor type you think would complement the dish. There are no wrong answers, only experiments!

Once you know the general flavor profile, you can pick a few herbs to add. If you are a beginner, I would recommend adding only one herb (or two at most), so you can get a feel for how they influence the taste. After all, if you add all of your herbs to everything, it will all start to taste the same.

Finally, check the Cheat Sheets for each herb to see what types of dishes they usually work best in (soup, poultry, seafood, etc.), how to add them (dry or fresh, before or after cooking), and the type of flavor they will add (floral, spicy, citrus, etc.). There can be a substantial difference in flavor (and amounts used in recipes) between fresh and dry herbs. While most herbs can be used fresh, I have highlighted the herbs that can just as easily be used dry when cooked. A general rule of thumb is that herbs with more woody stems and stiffer leaves work better dried compared to softer, more delicate herbs, which tend to lose all of their flavors when dried out or overcooked.

Nothing in this section will be correct all of the time, and cooking is full of exceptions, but these can be seen as general rules of thumb to follow as you're learning.

One rule that doesn't have an exception is always to remember and remove herb stems or inedible leaves (like bay leaves or raw sage) before serving. These can be very unpleasant to bite into.

What flavor profile are you working with?

Depending on what type of herb garden you planted, you might have most or all of the flavors needed to create cuisines from around the world. Generally, the flavors of herbs in these categories go well with each other.

However, you will almost certainly have to supplement with spices and other additions. Here is a quick summary of the flavors you would need to re-create some popular cooking styles.

The Essesntial Herb Gardening Handbook

Herbs	Italian	French	Spanish	Mediter-ranean	Mexican	Indian/Asian	African
Basil	X					X	
Bay Leaf	X		X	X			
Chives	X	X				X	
Cilantro				X	X	X	
Dill				X			
Fennel		X		X			
Garlic	X		X		X	X	
Marjoram	X	X					
Mint				X	X	X	
Oregano			X	X	X		
Parsley		X		X			
Rosemary	X	X					
Sage	X	X					
Summer Savory		X					
Tarragon		X		X			
Thyme	X	X		X	X		
Winter Savory		X					
Supplementary Flavors							
Allspice					X	X	
Berbere							X
Chervil		X					
Chili pepper			X				
Cinnamon					X	X	
Cloves			X		X	X	X
Coconut						X	X
Cumin					X	X	
Ginger						X	
Grains of Paradise							X
Harissa							X
Lemon grass						X	
Mastic				X			
Nutmeg			X	X		X	
Olives			X	X			
Paprika			X		X		X
Per-peri							X
Pimentón			X				
Saffron			X				
Sesame						X	
Turmeric						X	
Vanilla					X		
Zanzibar							X

Herb Cooking Cheat Sheets

Basil

How to use: Fresh or raw

Types of dishes: soups, salads, seafood, meat, poultry, vegetables, eggs, cheeses

When to add: after cooking is complete or just before serving

Flavor description: strong and sharp, can be slightly peppery and sweet

Bay Leaf

How to use: Fresh or dried (fresh Bay leaves are very potent but do not last long)

Types of dishes: soups, seafood, meat, poultry, vegetables

When to add: before cooking, then removed before serving

Flavor description: very subtle minty-peppery flavor that is used more as an enhancement to proteins and sauces rather than a distinct flavor of it's own

The Essesntial Herb Gardening Handbook

CELERY

How to use: fresh or raw

Types of dishes: soups, salads, meat, poultry

When to add: before or after cooking (cooking removes the bitter flavor)

Flavor description: Adds a salty or onion-like flavor that can be spicy and slightly bitter

CHIVES

How to use: fresh or raw

Types of dishes: soups, salads, poultry, vegetables, eggs, cheeses

When to add: just before serving, typically as a garnish

Flavor description: very mild and slightly sweet onion flavor

CILANTRO

How to use: fresh

Types of dishes: soups, salads, seafood, meat, desserts

When to add: after cooking is complete or just before serving

Flavor description: bright citrus flavor

Note: some people get an unpleasant soap-like taste from cilantro, unfortunately this is genetic and there is nothing to remedy it, these people will just have to avoid cilantro

Dill

How to use: fresh

Types of dishes: soup, salad, seafood, poultry, vegetables, eggs, cheeses

When to add: near the end or after cooking

Flavor description: grassy and sweet with mild hint of licorice

Note: flavor changes quite a bit (for the worse) after flowering

Fennel

How to use: fresh

Types of dishes: soups, salad, seafood, meat

When to add: before or after cooking

Flavor description: sharper and stronger licorice flavor than dill, that becomes much milder and sweeter after being cooked

Garlic

How to use: fresh or roasted

Types of dishes: put in everything but dessert, if a dish is missing something, it probably needs garlic

When to add: before cooking

Flavor description: Earthy, warm, and savory, becomes sweeter after cooking or roasting

The Essesntial Herb Gardening Handbook

Lavender

How to use: fresh

Types of dishes: soups, salads, desserts

When to add: before cooking

Flavor description: sweet and floral

Lemon Balm

How to use: fresh

Types of dishes: salads, desserts, teas (can use as a substitute for mint)

When to add: before or after cooking

Flavor description: bright and citrus

Marjoram

How to use: fresh or dried

Types of dishes: soups, salads, meat, poultry, vegetables, eggs, cheeses (can use as a substitute for oregano or thyme)

When to add: before or after cooking

Flavor description: woody and floral, milder than oregano and sweeter than thyme

Mint

How to use: fresh

Types of dishes: salads, meat, eggs, cheeses, desserts

When to add: before (dried) or after cooking, or just before serving (fresh)

Flavor description: sharp and sweet, producing a cooling effect on the tongue, there are countless varieties, each with their own subtle differences

Oregano

How to use: fresh or dried

Types of dishes: soups, salads, seafood, meat, poultry, vegetables, eggs, cheeses

When to add: before cooking, heat removes the bitterness

Flavor description: aromatic, earthy, and slightly bitter

Parsley

How to use: fresh, but it does not keep well once cut

Types of dishes: soups, salads, seafood, poultry

When to add: after cooking or just before serving

Flavor description: very mild and clean, peppery flavor that is just bitter enough to balance out sweet dishes

The Essesntial Herb Gardening Handbook

Rosemary

How to use: fresh or dried

Types of dishes: seafood, meat, poultry, vegetables, cheeses

When to add: before cooking

Flavor description: strong pine tree or evergreen-like woody flavor

Sage

How to use: fresh or dried

Types of dishes: soups, meat

When to add: near the end of cooking, often removed before serving

Flavor description: savory and pine

Savory

How to use: fresh or dried

Types of dishes: soups, meat, vegetables

When to add: before cooking

Flavor description: sweet, spicy and peppery

Tarragon

How to use: fresh

Types of dishes: salads, seafood, poultry, vegetables, eggs, cheeses

When to add: near the end of cooking (becomes bitter with heat)

Flavor description: sweet and bitter with hints of vanilla and licorice

Thyme

How to use: fresh or dried

Types of dishes: soups, salads, meat, poultry, vegetables

When to add: before or after cooking

Flavor description: sweet and savory, like a milder version of oregano

Conclusion

Congratulations, you have all the tools you need to plan, grow, harvest, and use your own herbs.

Remember to share your successes, learn from your mistakes, and enjoy every moment!

A Special Gift Just for You

Use my **'Outdoor Space Planner'** to:

- Get inspired, and choose what elements you *like*, *want*, or *need* to have in your new outdoor space
- Identify any special requirements or restrictions that might be roadblocks to improving your backyard or balcony
- Create an easy to follow budget so you don't run out of money, space, or time
- Draw out your personalized design and plan a schedule for everything to get delivered, built, and installed.

Go to https://www.subscribepage.com/danielistein to get it now!

Glossary

Acidic: This usually refers to the type of soil. Some plants prefer acidic soil to grow. See PH below.

Alkaline: This usually refers to the type of soil. See PH below.

Annual: This is a plant which you sow, it grows and then dies back in one year.

Biennial: This is a plant that is sown and grows well in year 1 but flowers in year 2. It has a 2-year cycle and usually tried to go to seed in year 2.

Compost: This can be purchased or made by you as a free homemade resource, often called "Black Gold" by experienced gardeners. See how to make your own by recycling any household vegetable and fruit waste, combining it with paper waste and thicker twigs from your garden pruning to make an excellent plant fertilizer for your garden, herbs, and fruit trees. See Chapter 5.

Crop rotation: A growing system that is used to ensure that soil does not get depleted by growing the same crop in the same loca-

Glossary

tion every year. This helps to produce healthy soil and reduce pests. See Chapter 7.

Drying herbs: how to do this. See Lemon Balm in Chapter 6.

Green manure: also called a cover crop, is withered or dying plant material that is added as a soil amendment. Any green plant material that hasn't decomposed is green manure.

Harden off: This is when your new seedlings are placed outdoors during the day to get them used to being outdoors and then taken back indoors overnight. They are getting used to being outdoors.

Leaf mold: This is a process to use any leftover, dropped leaves in the fall. It is a free resource that provided bulk for soil and can be used in potting plants on.

NPK feeds: These plant foods are sold in gardening stores and they provide 3 critical nutrients for plants.

- N is for nitrogen which makes healthy leaves.
- P is for phosphorus which makes healthy roots.
- K is for potassium or potash which is essential for flowers, keeps the stem healthy, and allows your herb to use nitrogen.

PH of soil: The PH of soil measures the contents on a scale. Soil types vary, depending on the underlying stone formation, usage of the soil in the past, etc.

- Soil with a PH from 6.5 to 7.5 is *neutral*.
- Soil with a PH of less than 6.5 is *acidic*. Any soil less than 5.5 is strongly acidic.
- Soil with a PH of more than 7.5 is *alkaline*.

Glossary

The soil you choose will depend on the needs of your particular herbs. You can buy composts made for ericaceous plants, which like acid soil and a normal grow bag will be quite fertile with a balance of nutrients. Check what soil your herbs enjoys before planting and check the PH with a testing kit if you are not sure.

Propagation: To sow seeds, to divide plants that become too leggy, and to take cuttings to make new plants or to ensure plants for the following year. See Chapter 7.

Perennial: This is a plant that lives for many years. It is sown and grows steadily to become a small shrub, or even a tree. Chapter 1.

Pests: which attack herbs such as aphids, caterpillars, earwigs, greenflies, slugs, snails, whitefly, red spider mite, scale insects. See Chapter 7.

Root rot: refers to a condition where healthy roots become pot-bound or waterlogged leading to brown, diseased roots. Healthy roots should be white or cream. See Chapter 6.

Self-seeding: is exactly as described. The plant completes its growth cycle, makes flowers, then seeds and these seeds fall on the ground so that you do not need to plant them. Once the seedlings show, you can move them easily, if you need to.

www.ingramcontent.com/pod-product-compliance
Lightning Source LLC
Chambersburg PA
CBHW031113080526
44587CB00011B/961